Retirement Harvest

A Guide for the Fall and Winter of Life

By Kenneth Stephenson

Dedication

This book is dedicated to:

My best friend and wife, Sandy. You've been there for me since
the beginning of this amazing journey and
have always been my biggest cheerleader.

My children, Colt and Ashlee. You've seen your dad grow this
business almost from the start with struggles and victories.

My parents. For instilling a work ethic that
the farm life brings.

My staff. For supporting me, day in and day out.

Kenneth D. Stephenson is a ChFC® and CFEd®. He is also President and Chief Investment Advisor of Quest 10 Wealth Builders, Inc. a registered investment adviser.

Kenneth is also president/owner of Complete Financial Solutions, Inc. which markets annuities and other insurance products. The information presented by the author and the publisher is for information and educational purposes only. It should not be considered specific investment advice, does not take into consideration your specific situation, and does not intend to make an offer or solicitation for the sale or purchase of any securities or investment strategies. Additionally no legal or tax advice is being offered. If legal or tax advice is needed a qualified professional should be engaged. Investments involve risk and are not guaranteed. This book contains information that might be dated and is intended only to educate and entertain. Any links or websites referred to are for informational purposes only.

Websites not associated with the author are unaffiliated sources of information and the author takes no responsibility for the accuracy of the information provided by these websites. Be sure to consult with a qualified financial adviser and/or tax professional before implementing any strategy discussed herein.

Table of Contents

Preface

Just as acres of cornfields grow from the smallest of seeds, the idea to write this book began with a kernel of thought I had shortly after the stock market crash of 2008. As a financial advisor who specializes in retirement planning, I was on the front line. The Dow Jones Industrial Average, which most people watch as a barometer of the nation's economic health, closed at 14,164.43 on October 9, 2007. Less than 18 months later, on March 5, 2009, it had fallen more than 50% to 6,594.44. The worst single day was on September 29, 2008, when the Dow plunged a record 777 points.

No one was calling it a depression, but plenty of people were depressed about what was happening. Many hard-working Americans who had saved all their lives for their retirement saw as much as half of their savings vanish like dandelion spores in a wind gust. Recession, depression – those are only words made up by economists. I like what former president Harry S. Truman said: "It's a recession when your neighbor loses **his** job; it's a depression when you lose **your own.**"

Because I work primarily with clients who are retired or approaching retirement, I advocate only safe-money investments and low-risk strategies. None of my clients were wiped out by the 2008 crash. But I heard about it from many with whom I met subsequently to help them salvage what was left of their portfolios and work to rebuild. Many were hurt both financially and psychologically. Some were angry, wanting to know why their broker hadn't warned them that such a thing could happen. Many were even told that it would not happen to them. This upset me and is another reason why I decided to write this book. Others were understandably distrustful of a system they believed had failed them. In many of those conversations, I sensed that people wanted answers. I knew I couldn't write a book that would prevent another market crash, or stave off another recession. Andrew Sorkin, in his New York Times bestseller *Too Big to Fail,* points out that the biggest players in the financial world, including the Federal Reserve, say they expect these periods (referring to the 2008 Wall Street collapse) to come along every six to 10 years. Doesn't it make sense that if even the government knows these things are coming, you should prepare for them as well?

Economic catastrophes are like natural weather phenomena. They occur because of slowly developing economic forces that eventually come to a head. Sort of like hurricanes that form in the Atlantic because of heat waves coming off the African desert. You can't stop those. They just happen. But what you **can** do is point out to a friend the danger of building a home in a flood plain. That's what this book is about – steps you can take at various stages of your life to ensure you have a comfortable and worry-free retirement and are not a victim of economic forces over which you have no control.

Statistically, the Great Recession cost the American economy approximately $10 trillion and 8 million jobs. But those are just numbers. The fallout was up close and personal for those who experienced the actual losses. One couple with whom I worked following the crash – John and Joann, we will call them – were both 57 years old and had plans to retire in their early 60s. The couple both had what one would classify as steady, dependable jobs working for the telephone company. They had worked diligently and contributed regularly to their 401(k) retirement programs. Like many, they paid little attention to the investments within their retirement accounts. They preferred to let someone else handle all of that for them, and they asked few questions. John and Joann figured that in three or four more years they would retire and begin living off their savings. Between that and their Social Security checks, they figured they could life in relative comfort for the rest of their lives, perhaps even do some traveling. Then 2008 happened.

John and Joann said they had grown accustomed to trusting other people to make their money decisions for them.

"We would just open the statements and glance at them," John said. "As long as the number at the bottom right-hand corner was higher than it was the month before, we were satisfied."

Joann said that even though they were on the threshold of retirement, no one had bothered to tell them they had too much of their portfolio at risk in equities. As a consequence, the couple lost nearly half their life savings. On Wednesday, September 17, 2008, the Dow Jones Industrial Average fell 449 points and money market funds lost $144 billion. They were told to "just hang in there because the market will bounce back." Who were they to question the "professionals"? Sure enough, there were signs in the next few days that gave them some encouragement. But their hopes were dashed when a few days later, the Dow fell that record 777 points to hit a new low of 7,552.29.

Our team set to work trying to stop the bleeding and forged a plan to salvage what was left. The first order of business was to get their money out of harm's way. They were too close to retirement to have what was left of their life savings riding on the chancy roulette wheel the stock market had become. The second priority was to position their retirement savings where they could get a steady and reasonable rate of return and lastly provide the couple with a guaranteed income that would last them for the rest of their lives. John and Joann knew they would have to make some adjustments in their plans in order to get to the retirement income level they wanted. They each decided to work an extra four years to make up for some of what they had lost. It wasn't what they wanted, but it was better than what they had expected. They were smiling when we finished hammering out the plan, and it made me feel good to know I had been able to help them. But for the rest of that week, I couldn't get the "what if's" off my mind. "What if" I could have met them a few years, or even a few months before the market crash? What if I could have explained to them some of the safe-money alternatives that many of my existing clients employed to avoid unnecessary market risk? They could have realized the early retirement for which they had so arduously worked and eagerly awaited. But the past was past. As my father used to say, "That cow was already out of the barn." The damage this couple experienced was done. But how many others could I perhaps reach if I could put into book form the message I would have given to John and Joann had I been afforded the opportunity?

If it is true what they say about history – that it repeats itself and that those who do not learn lessons from the past are doomed to repeat it – then perhaps a larger audience could benefit. Of course, some will never learn. As my mother used to say: "They don't believe powder will burn." Much of the financial hardship imposed on those who lost money during 2008 market crash could have been prevented by simply applying the principles of safe-money investing and risk control you will see presented in the pages of this book. The ideas, examples and case studies compiled here are intended to help you through all the phases of your financial lives.

If you are wondering about some of the farming metaphors you'll see here, both in the title of this book and liberally sprinkled throughout its pages, let me explain that I come by them honestly. I learned from my father how to plant, plow, cultivate, reap, tend livestock and perform every kind of work that growing up on a working farm demanded of a young boy. As a matter of fact, I still live on the farm that my father and mother, Charles and Ruth Stephenson, started tending shortly after they were married. The rich, sandy soil that covers the land where the Inner Coastal Plan and the Piedmont regions of North Carolina meet makes for some of the best farm land this side of the Mississippi. And while I no longer do the day-to-day work of raising crops and livestock, I still consider myself a farmer by heritage. I learned much about nature and about life in general from working on a farm.

As you may know, harvest time is a time of celebration in rural America. Your labors throughout the year are about to finally produce fruit. You have sown well, kept the weeds and bugs away, and you have adhered to the science of agriculture, some of which you learned on your own but most of which came from tried and tested methods passed down to you by others. And now it is time to gather and preserve, and to enjoy the fall and winter, secure in the knowledge that you have done your best. Pumpkins on the porch and hay bales (or balls, as they are configured now) in the fields mean the hard work is over and a time of relaxation and enjoyment is to follow.

That is the kind of bountiful harvest I wish for you.

Part One

Spring

Chapter One

Planting for the Future

"The sluggard will not plow by reason of the cold; [therefore] shall he beg in harvest, and [have] nothing." ~ Proverbs 20:4

I couldn't help but chuckle the other day when I was perusing a U.S. Bureau of Labor Statistics website page on farming. I wanted to find out how many farmers there were in America. I did find the answer – approximately 1.8 million. But that wasn't what I found amusing. Stated quite matter-of-factly was this little piece of information: *"Farming can be hard work."* Yep! You got that right. I think farmers invented the phrase "daylight to dark." From the time I was old enough to be useful to my father on the farm, I remember getting out of bed before sunrise, pulling on my work clothes and helping him perform the many chores that demanded our attention. I look back on that as one of the most valuable life lessons ever learned – hard work is, well, *hard.* But it won't kill you. I am living proof of that.

In the spring, the planting of crops was the first order of business. Tobacco was the cash crop, but we also grew corn, soybeans and vegetables. Prior to planting, the land had to be disked, plowed and then dragged so it was flat and smooth for planting. I remember standing on the back of an old grain seeder to make sure the seeds flowed freely and made their way into the soil. Obviously, without planting, there would be no crop to harvest.

It is like that with our financial lives. The soil is prepared when we are getting an education and preparing for our careers, whatever they may turn out to be. This "soil preparation" is not as easy as it used to be. Education is free until we graduate high school. Then, depending on what manner of higher education you choose, it can cost you dearly. College is not a prerequisite for success.

According to *USA Today*, the average tuition at a four-year public university rose 15% between 2008 and 2010. The College Board, a not-for-profit research organization formerly known as the College Entrance Examination Board, reports that a "moderate" college budget for an in-state public college for the 2012–2013 academic year averaged $22,261. A moderate budget at a private college averaged $43,289. That's just **one year,** folks. Multiply that by four to get the average cost of a four-year education, of course, but a growing number of students are spending six years at university before claiming their degrees.

Is it any wonder student loan debt racked up in the past decade or so finally eclipsed credit card debt? In November 2012, the Federal Reserve Bank of New York reported that student loan debt increased to $956 billion, more than auto loan debt or credit card debt. More worrisome, said the report, was that the delinquency rate on student loans has reached serious proportions. In other words, people aren't paying back their loans on time and some skip out on them entirely.

So why is education costing more? First of all, there is tuition, the money you pay the college or university just to go and be taught there. Then add fees for the ancillary services that go with the above, such as internet access, parking, library access, bus service...the list goes on and on. Unless you live close enough to an institution of higher learning to stay at home while you learn, you will have to pay for room and board, meals and other miscellany associated with the college experience. Oh, and don't forget books. You will need those. The College Board reports the average cost for books and supplies for the 2012–2013 school year was $1,200 at public colleges and $1,244 at private colleges.

I'm not telling you all of this, young readers, to scare you or talk you out of getting a college degree. In fact, I strongly encourage you to prepare yourself for life by getting all the education you possibly can. These costs may seem overwhelming, but there are ways to keep expenses down. Remember that college educations come at all levels of cost, and that **financial aid** can reduce that cost. If a school is a great fit for you but seems too expensive, it makes sense to apply and then see whether your financial aid offer will bring the cost down. In other words, don't give up on a college just because of the sticker price. That's not the end of the story.

First of all, financial aid is not a form of welfare. Financial aid is (a) your tax dollars at work and (b) the system's way of helping deserving applicants qualify for the education they are entitled to. Many students from lower-income and middle-income families do not apply for financial aid because they mistakenly think that their income is too high or that they can't afford college. For many families, however, financial aid is the major source of money for college. Financial aid can come from the federal government, from the state government or from the college itself. It can include scholarships (which you don't have to repay), loans (which you do have to repay), and work-study (which helps you pay for college out of your earnings). The key is, however, that you must apply for the aid. As deserving as you may be, the institutions that provide financial aid for higher education cannot read your mind and will not chase you down.

How to Apply For Financial Aid

Colleges base financial aid eligibility on a calculation of what a family should be able to pay toward college costs, called the Expected Family Contribution (EFC). The difference between the EFC and actual college costs (as determined by the college) is the family's "financial need." Colleges try to cover this need with financial aid, either through government aid or their own institutional aid.

The first thing students (and those helping them) have to do to start this process is determine what type of financial aid applications you will have to complete. You won't be eligible for financial aid unless you complete the **FAFSA,** the Free Application for Federal Student Aid. The easiest way to do this is to go online and fill it out, at the

www.fasfa.ed.gov website. The earliest you can fill out the form is
January 1 of each year, but keep in mind your tax return information is
often needed to complete it. The student must obtain a PIN, which will
be necessary to electronically sign the FAFSA form and retrieve the
family's financial aid records. Filling out the FAFSA is a must for
anyone who hopes to receive financial help from federal or state
programs, as well as need-based aid from colleges themselves. Federal
Student Aid is an office of the U.S. Department of Education, and, as
is the case with any government agency or office, there is a measure of
complexity to dealing with all of this. But if going through the research
and filling out the forms means the difference between you getting an
education or settling for a permanent job at the local car wash, don't
you think it's worth it?

It is just my observation, but high school guidance counselors must
be stretched pretty thin these days because I am surprised at how
many parents with college-bound children don't know their way
through this maze. For example, many are not aware that in order to
complete a FAFSA profile, they must first register with the College
Board. Students are registered if they have taken the Scholastic
Aptitude Test (SAT). It is also critical to make sure to meet the
financial aid deadline of the schools where you are applying. They
won't hold the bus for you if you miss it. There is a lot of competition
for financial aid, and the early bird often gets the worm.

Speaking of starting college planning early, I recommend that
families start planning for college as early as junior high school. The
last I heard, merit scholarships are given to kids with good grades.
Start taking those grades seriously when your children are in junior
high school. It could mean thousands of dollars to your family (and to
the student if money is borrowed). Can students study for the SAT
tests? Absolutely! There are websites and computer programs galore
that tutor them on how to score high on the SATs. If necessary, hire a
tutor. Think of those numbers as dollars.

Get proactive in your search for grants and scholarships.
Scholarships are granted to students based on such things as merit,
athleticism, religion and ethnicity, among other criteria. Virtually
all colleges, the state where your student goes to school and the federal

government provide students with thousands of scholarships from which to choose. Lists for these scholarships can be found with a college adviser, online or at a high school career guidance office. There are hundreds of millions of dollars in scholarship monies available in the United States. Much of this "free money" goes unclaimed because people don't turn over enough stones looking for the opportunities.

Strategies for the FAFSA

FAFSA forms are pretty straightforward. They want to know how much your family makes and how much your family owns. They go by your last year's tax return. If you are contemplating sending a son or daughter to college, why not do a trial FAFSA just to see what questions are asked and see how your assets balance against financial aid requirements? It may surprise you to know that there are "reportable" assets and "non-reportable" assets. At this writing, annuities and cash value life insurance are in the "non-reportable" category, while stocks, bonds, real estate and cash are in the "reportable" category. That is a broad generalization. Always seek the advice of a financial planner with knowledge of these matters before making financial decisions.

All things considered, then, the harvest we anticipate reaping begins with preparing the soil for the eventual sowing of the seeds of that harvest. Education is the primary building block for that endeavor and must be pursued.

Chapter Two

Work Is Fundamental

"I'm glad I don't have to make a living farming.
Too much hard work. Too many variables
you don't have control over, like, is it
going to rain? All I can say is, God bless
the real farmers out there."
~ Fuzzy Zoeller

What I am about to tell you is something that, if you are older, you already know. If you are in your middle years, you are probably living it. If you are in your late teens and early 20s, you probably don't want to hear about it, but in the back of your mind you know it to be true: If you want to have a worry-free retirement – full of freedom and fun – you must **work hard now and save as much money as you can.**

Successful people in every field are often said to be "blessed with talent" or even just lucky. But those who enjoy that success will tell you the harder they worked, the luckier they got.

Retirement is probably the last thing on your mind if you're a young person. And that is understandable. Youth is a time when you are full of energy and bright promise. So if you are a young reader and you are still on this page, you are to be commended for extending your interest span. When you are just jumping on the merry-go-round of life, it is hard to imagine that there will come a point in this great adventure when you will want to slow things down and jump off. But – and you will have to trust me on this – it will come sooner than you think. The sooner you start thinking about the future, the better. Even more said, the sooner you start **working** toward the future the better. From where I watch the world, the ones who succeed are the ones who work the hardest and persist with the most determination.

One of my favorite quotes is from the 30th president of the United States, Calvin Coolidge. History doesn't regard him as being a world shaker. He was president during the roaring 20s and is best known for his taciturnity. Because he had little to say about anything, he was nicknamed Silent Cal, Cool Cal, Cautious Cal and the Sphinx of the Potomac. Let's just say that if he were alive today he probably wouldn't sign up for a Twitter account. But Mr. Coolidge did leave behind one of the most profound comments ever uttered about that simple ingredient of the human spirit in which he deeply believed – persistence. The quote goes like this:

> *"Nothing in the world can take the place of Persistence. Talent will not; nothing is more common than unsuccessful men with talent. Genius will not; unrewarded genius is almost a proverb. Education will not; the world is full of educated derelicts. Persistence and determination alone are omnipotent."*

While modern presidents have handlers and speech writers at their beck and call, it seems that "Silent Cal" actually penned those words. And they are true indeed. In this book, I have the luxury of tossing thousands of words out there as road signs that ultimately point to success. And you will see many of them as you read on. But if I were limited to just one word, it would be **WORK**. Not saving? Not investing? Not education? Those things are important, but hard work trumps them all if you have to choose.

Basketball Superstar Michael Jordan

Because I live in a part of North Carolina that is within easy driving distance to where Michael Jordan played high school basketball (Emsley A. Laney High School in Wilmington) and college basketball (University of North Carolina at Chapel Hill), I have had a unique vantage point from which to watch his career unfold. Now, of course, he is legendary for his prowess as a player, having earned the title in the estimation of most sports analysts as the greatest basketball player to have ever played the game. What many do not know is how hard MJ had to work at the game to be that good.

In 1978, Michael Jordan, the pro player who led the Chicago Bulls to six NBA championships in the late 1980s and early 1990s, was just plain old Mike Jordan, a lanky sophomore player for Coach Clifton "Pop" Herring's Laney High School Buccaneers. In fact, one of the most infamous roster decisions in high school basketball history was when the gangling young Jordan was relegated to the junior varsity, even though other sophomores were chosen to play varsity ball. Why? Because his shooting was described as "good but not great," and his defensive effort was considered by the coach to be "mediocre." Those who knew Jordan in those days said he distinguished himself during tryouts and practices by being first in line for the conditioning drills and would run harder than anyone, even running extra laps after the whistle sounded just because he wanted to work hard to improve. In all fairness to his former high school coach, the 15-year-old Jordan was only 5'10" at the time, and "Pop" Herring believed in giving the seniors top billing on the varsity squad, but he will still go down in history as the coach who cut Michael Jordan.

A *Sports Illustrated* story that appeared January 16, 2012, entitled, "Did This Man Really Cut Michael Jordan?" pointed out that ironically the handwritten list that cut MJ from the roster was posted on the door to the building that would later be renamed Michael J. Jordan Gymnasium. According to the article, when Jordan saw his name on the list of those not selected on the varsity, he went home and cried. But in fact, his name was on the second list, the JV roster, with the names of many of his fellow sophomores. Jordan didn't quit because of the setback. In fact, he quickly became a JV superstar.

"He was so good, in fact, that the jayvee games became quite popular," David Halberstam wrote in his 1999 biography of Jordan, *Playing for Keeps*. "The entire varsity began to come early so they could watch him play in the jayvee games." Jordan became determined to work harder than ever so that he would never be cut again. As a college player, Jordan was an instant success at UNC-Chapel Hill during the 1981-82 season, earning Atlantic Coast Conference freshman of the year honors and famously sinking the game-winning shot in the national title game against Georgetown that year. In his three seasons with the Tar Heels, he averaged 17.7 points per game and shot 54 percent from the field, winning the Wooden and Naismith player of the year awards as a junior. All of that is in the record books. What you won't see there, however, is his work ethic. He wanted his body in perfect physical shape. He spent hours in the weight room after practice. After everyone else had left the building, he stayed and worked on his shooting technique for hours. According to his long-time coach with the Chicago Bulls, Phil Jackson, it was hard work that made him a legend. "When Jordan first entered the league, his jump shot wasn't good enough," Halberstam quoted Jackson. "He spent his off season taking hundreds of jumpers a day until it was perfect."

GE CEO Jeff Immelt

Because more people are interested in basketball than they are business, hardworking business executives are not so likely to be in the limelight as high-profile athletes. But General Electric CEO Jeff Immelt is on the same level among corporation heads as basketball great Michael Jordan is among famous sports figures. Immelt is called "The Bionic Manager" because of his work ethic and machine-like stamina. It is said about Immelt that he could work 100 hours a week for 24 years with no apparent ill effects. Immelt is smack-dab in the middle of the baby boom generation (those born between 1946 and 1964) and is age 56 as this book is written. But the word on the street is that he gets up at 5:30 a.m. each day for a cardio workout, during which he reads the papers and watches CNBC. He spends 30% of his workweek evaluating people, 30% in operations, 30% on growth initiatives and 10% on governance, investor communications and board communications.

Commenting on Immelt's work ethic, *CNN Money* magazine quoted his brother, Steve Immelt, as saying: "He works pretty hard at making it look easy. When we were kids he'd sneak away–to study."

That was when they were growing up in Cincinnati, where their father was a 38-year GE employee, a middle manager in the aircraft-engine business. Even in high school, Jeff was always busy – football, basketball, baseball, great grades. Brother Steve says, "Today it looks easy because he's working his butt off in a way you don't see." When asked to summarize the secret of his success, Immelt said, "There are 24 hours in a day, and you can use all of them."

Since taking over as GE Chief Executive Officer in 2000, Immelt has been named one of the "World's Best CEOs" three times by Barron's, and since he began serving as chief executive officer, GE has been named "America's Most Admired Company" in a poll conducted by *Fortune* magazine and one of "The World's Most Respected Companies" in polls by *Barron's* and the *Financial Times*.

Charles Davis Stephenson

Born June 13, 1928, in rural Johnson County, North Carolina, Charles Stephenson had to drop out of school in the eighth grade to come home and work on the farm. It was just what many young boys did in those days after they learned how to read and figure. For a farm family to survive the Depression, they needed "all hands on deck," so to speak. If you were healthy enough to work, then you worked, most often from dawn until dark. Charles is a member of that stalwart generation who lived through the Great Depression and never had anything handed to him, except maybe the handle of a hoe or a shovel when his young hands were large enough to grasp them and put them to use on the farm.

Charles went into the Army in July 1946 at the age of 18 and served there for approximately four years. When he came home, he met his soon-to-be-bride, Mamie Ruth Stephenson, almost right away. They were married in 1950. Since farming was all he knew, he began farming again, this time as a "share cropper," the designation given to someone who farmed someone else's land and gave them a share of the crops as payment. For the next 20 or so years, until the 1970s, Charles worked tirelessly with one goal in mind – to buy and own

18

outright the land he had been farming for the last two decades. It was prime farmland and would be perfect for growing the crops like tobacco, corn, soybeans and wheat that Charles had in mind.

If there was a way to make money farming, Charles would find out what it was. As time went by, he maintained a small hog operation and raised beef cattle too. Tobacco was the cash crop throughout North Carolina in those days and Charles raised his share.

In 1966, Charles and Ruth Stephenson built a home. Despite a full workload on the farm, Charles traveled to Raleigh, the nearest big city, and worked at tearing down old homes in the wintertime to earn extra money with which to build the new home. If he saw good lumber that was going to be discarded anyway, he would haul it back to southern Wake County and use it as building materials for his new house. The way he looked at it, every dollar saved was a dollar earned, and he was getting paid twice for his work. In addition to being paid for demolishing old buildings, he was using the

Kenneth's parents, Charles and Ruth Stephenson, in 1950.

salvageable lumber for sheds, barns and outbuildings he needed on the farm. Some of the wood used to build the historic old cotton gin that stood for years on Highway 55 in Angier, North Carolina, was later used to build some of the farm buildings that Charles erected after the cotton gin's demolition.

Charles also worked in the winter pouring concrete driveways. He volunteered to do carpenter work for the elderly. After buying the farm in southern Wake County, he started a firewood business. There were 50 acres of wooded land that had to be cleared and made arable for crops. No sense letting that wood go to waste when there were plenty of people in nearby Raleigh who would pay good money to burn it in their fireplaces.

As much as he believed in the old-fashioned values of hard work and saving what you made, Charles was also a progressive thinker. He was one of the first farmers in the area to use automated tobacco harvesters, an idea he began implementing in 1975 that is used almost exclusively today.

Charles was also a devout family man, having served for many years at the Fellowship Baptist Church in Willow Spring, North Carolina, as a deacon and then as a trustee. He led the rebuilding of the church in 1992 after a fire destroyed the first one and still regards that as the single accomplishment in which he takes the most pride. The congregation had a goal to re-open the church on Thanksgiving Day, less than a year from the time of the fire. Charles stayed on top of the project and, although it was a daunting task, a Thanksgiving service was conducted in the new building to the delight of all the parishioners.

No, Charles Stephenson will never be listed as one of the world's wealthiest or most powerful men. But in my view – and I admit to being a bit prejudiced here since he is my father – he epitomizes the principles of thrift, hard work and making the best out of the hand that life deals you. At the time of this writing, my father lives with Mamie Ruth, my mother and his bride of 64 years in an assisted living facility. He was diagnosed with Alzheimer's disease in 2005. And although I have acknowledged my possible bias, he is still a perfect example – at least the best one I can think of – to show that with hard work, dedication and the love of one's family, one can accomplish big things no matter the station of life from which you came.

Elmer W. Smidlap III

What's that? You've never heard of Elmer W. Smidlap III? Well, that's understandable. You see, Elmer was one of those people who never accomplished very much in life because **he didn't work.** In fact, the only thing Elmer is famous for is for coining the sardonic phrase: "I just love work...I could watch it all day long." On a test in high school, when asked to define the term "manual labor," he tentatively wrote "President of Mexico." Naturally, he failed the test. Poor Elmer. No wonder you never hear of him.

The point is – and the world is full of examples of this – **work leads to success.** Inventor Thomas Edison put it this way: "Genius is one percent inspiration and 99 percent perspiration."

I can honestly say that, although I learned much from the university training I received after high school, I place a greater value on the "work ethics" degree I earned on the farm. One of the many lessons learned from working with the land was that hard work won't kill you. As a matter of fact, it makes you physically fit and better equipped psychologically to deal with the challenges of the adult world.

It teaches you how to ardently pursue a goal. Life on the farm was a much better teacher in that respect than any of my college instructors could have been. At harvest time, we took advantage of the daylight from the moment it made its gauzy, pink appearance through the long-leaf pines until it said an orange goodnight over the opposite horizon, and were never the worse for the wear. There would be time to relax when the crops were in.

Wanting it All Now

Our world is filled with tools designed to satisfy our craving for immediacy – smart phones, instant text messages, high speed wireless internet, emails, overnight shipping, 24/7 news coverage. We seem to be the generation that screams into the mouth of our brimming cornucopia, "I want it all and I want it now!" That's one reason why scam artists succeed with get-rich-quick schemes and entry level jobs are shunned, even in an economy where unemployment is high. Far too many eager young people leave the doors of their alma mater, clutching their degrees, expecting the business world to welcome them with open arms and six-figure (or at least high five-figure) salaries. When reality sets in and they see that only the fortunate few who have burned the midnight oil and worked extremely hard are allowed through that narrow gate, they chuff at how unfair life is. And they're right. Life is patently unfair. There is nothing fair about it. The ones who succeed, however, don't look for breaks to come to them but strive to make their own breaks through that indomitable one-two punch of work and persistence.

That there is no dishonor in starting small, working hard and looking for opportunity can be seen in the histories that are now being written of wealthy Americans who were driven by dreams and propelled by their own industry and persistence to heralded success.

Oprah Winfrey, the daughter of an unwed teenage mother from rural Mississippi, is worth $2.8 billion. She conquered poverty, sexual abuse and her own teenage pregnancy to become a media mogul. She did all of this by maintaining a confident attitude. In her eponymous magazine *Oprah,* she writes: "What I know for sure is this – The big secret in life is that there is no big secret. Whatever your goal for this year is, you can get there—as long as you're willing to be honest with yourself about the preparation and work involved. There are no back doors, no free rides."

While still in high school, Winfrey landed a job at a local television station. She won a scholarship to Tennessee State University and would go on to work as a television news anchor in Baltimore and Nashville before landing her first talk show in Chicago. Within a few months, Winfrey had transformed AM Chicago from one of the city's lowest rated shows to the highest. Today, she is considered one of the richest and most influential women in the world – some say the most – and she got there through hard work.

Do Won Chang, a Korean immigrant, made his billions in the fashion industry. When he and his wife, Jin Sook, first arrived to America in 1981, Do Won had to work three jobs, janitor, gas station attendant and waiter in a coffee shop, just to make ends meet. But he worked hard, slept little and saved enough money to open a clothing store in 1984 called Fashion 21. That one store grew into Forever 21, which pioneered fast fashion and is now a multi-national chain of more than 480 stores generating around $300 billion per year. He has turned it into a family affair, with his daughter's Linda and Esther helping to run the company.

An article describing his success appeared in the July 31, 2010, issue of the *Los Angeles Times* in which reporter Ken Bensinger described Do Won as an entrepreneur with perseverance. "You can't go into business thinking that success will come to you in just one or two years," said Chang in the article, adding that success "is like a marathon, not a 100-meter dash."

For what it's worth, Chang is a religious man. His foundation is liberal with charitable donations to churches and other faith groups. He travels to perform missionary work and says the Bible is his favorite book. "Every Forever 21 shopping bag has a citation for a Bible verse printed on the bottom," he said.

Sam Walton (1918-1992) lived on a farm in Oklahoma during the Great Depression. In order to make ends meet, he helped his family out by milking cows and driving milk out to customers. He also delivered newspapers and sold magazine subscriptions. By 26, he was managing a variety store after graduating from the University of Missouri with a B.A. in economics. He used $5,000 from the army and a $20,000 loan from his father-in-law to buy a Ben Franklin variety store in Arkansas. He expanded the chain, and then went on to found Wal-Mart and Sam's Club. Walton did not amass his billions of dollars by being greedy and tricky, by swinging stock deals, gouging his customers or pyramiding bank loans. He succeeded by applying his own genius and hard work to the business of retailing, so that from one store in one small town he was able to build a chain of stores that now employs about 400,000 people. He was a plain man who drove an old pickup truck when he could have traveled in a chauffeured limousine, and preferred the Holiday Inn or similar hotel when he traveled. He contracted bone cancer and died in 1992, leaving the company to his wife and children. His name has become synonymous with hard work and persistence. His book *Sam Walton, Made in*

America by Sam Walton with John Huey (published by Doubleday) is worth the read.

I suppose, as they say when you are building a barn, "that nail is in the plank." We cannot know the future. Who knows? You just might win the lottery or accidently stumble upon a fortune. But probably not. So working hard and saving your money is still the best pathway to prosperity that I can recommend.

Chapter Three

Saving and Investing Early

"And God said, Behold, I have given you every
plant yielding seed that is on the face of all the
earth, and every tree with seed in its fruit. You shall
have them for food." ~ Genesis 1:29

It is amazing how many references there are to farming in the
Bible. That is only natural, I suppose, because most of the book was
originally written to those who worked the land, sowing and reaping,
tending to livestock. In the Old Testament, the cyclic principles of
"bearing seed" and fruit "with seed in it" were established early in the
book of Genesis. There are numerous references to farming, crops and
harvests in the words of the prophets to the ancient nation of Israel.
Not surprisingly, in the New Testament, many of Jesus' parables
involve the farming life. In all these references to sowing and reaping,
here are some of the principles we take away from the Good Book that
are true both agriculturally and financially:

Sowing and reaping involves waiting. Nothing good happens
overnight. A farmer must plant consistently and persistently and wait
for the crop to grow with the secure knowledge that "we shall reap if
we do not tire out."

We reap in proportion to what and how much we sow. When it
comes time to reap a harvest, it will be in proportion to what we
planted there. If we planted nothing, we will reap nothing and if we
planted little, we will reap little. "Whoever sows sparingly will also

reap sparingly, and whoever sows generously will also reap generously."

We reap *more* than what we sow. The law of sowing and reaping is related to the law of multiplication. In one parable, Jesus spoke of seed that brought forth "a hundred, sixty or thirty times what was sown" and how that "one grain of wheat produces a whole head of grain." In the same way, the time value of savings, while not realized at the time the money is saved, will be realized later on due to this principle of multiplication.

The Miracle of Compound Interest

The story goes that the great physicist Albert Einstein was asked, "What do you, Mr. Einstein, consider to be man's greatest invention?" He didn't say the wheel or the lever. He is reported to have said, "Compound interest." Whether he actually said this or not, we can agree that some of the greatest thinkers of our time understand the significance of compound interest. Another quote, sometimes attributed to Einstein, called compound interest the "eighth wonder of the world," and pointed out that "he who understands it earns it while he who doesn't, pays it."

The idea behind compound interest is transforming your working money into a dynamic, powerful income-generator. Compounding is when the earnings on an asset earn earnings, and those earnings earn still more earnings and on and on. It's like a snowball rolling downhill. The bigger it gets, the bigger it will get. Perhaps you have done that – rolled snow into a ball. The best time to do it is when there is about six inches of wet, sticky snow on the ground. You start with a fist-sized ball. At first the growth is slow. But seemingly before you know it, the ball is huge. Each turn of the snowy orb makes it grow upon itself until you can no longer move it. This is what usually turns into the bottom of a snowman if your childhood was anything like mine

It's like that with money. For compound interest to work two elements need to be in play – time and the reinvestment of earnings. The more time you give your investments (assuming there is no risk of loss), the more you are able to accelerate the growth and, as a consequence, the more income these investments produce. For example: If you invest, say, 10,000 today at 6%, you will have $10,600 in one year ($10,000 x 1.06). Let's say that instead of withdrawing the $600 you gained in interest, you leave it in the investment for another year. If you continue to get the same rate of interest, 6%, your account will grow to $11,236.00 ($10,600 x 1.06) by the end of the second year. Keep in mind, because you reinvested that $600 it works together with the original investment and you now earn $636 for that second year – $36 more than the year before. Big deal, right? Yes, it may seem like that now. But you just began rolling your snowball. Remember, you didn't do anything to earn that $36. It's extra money! And what is more, that $36 has the capacity to earn interest as well. The next year, your original investment of $10,000 will be worth $11,910 ($11,236 x 1.06). This time you earned $674.16, which is $74.16 more interest than the first year. This increase in the amount made each year is compounding in action: interest earning interest on interest and so on. This will continue as long as you keep reinvesting and earning interest.

The Value of Starting Early

Let's consider the case of John and Susan. They are both the same age. When Susan was 25 she put $15,000 into an account earning an interest rate of 5.5% For the sake of simple math, let's say that the interest rate was compounded annually. By the time Susan turns 50 years of age, she will have $57,200.89 ($15,000 x [1.055^25]) in her account. Not too shabby, eh?

But Susan's friend John waited another 10 years before he started investing. When he did, he invested the same amount as did Susan – $15,000 – and at the same interest rate of 5.5% compounded annually. By the time John turns 50, he will have $33,487.15 ($15,000 x [1.055^15]) in his account. Big difference! Why? Susan and John are both 50 years old, but Susan has $23,713.74 ($57,200.89 - $33,487.15) more than John even though they both invested the same amount of money. The reason is the **time** involved. By allowing more time for her investment to grow, Susan earned a total of $42,200.89 in interest while John only earned $18,487.15. It's amazing what a little time will do on the front end of a savings program when we are dealing with compound interest.

The time value of money is a fundamental concept in finance – and it influences every financial decision you make, whether you know it or not. I am going to propose something to you. And this is **not** a trick question, either, so don't over-think it. You have just won a prize of $10,000. Would you like the money now, or in three years? Of course you want it now, you answer instinctively. After all, a $100 bill today has the same value as a $100 bill one year from now. But that's not the end of the story. You can do much more with the money if you have it now because during those three years you can earn interest on your money. By investing that $10,000 immediately, you stand to increase the **future value** of your money. Unless they are paying you interest on that $10,000, there's no reason to wait.

As simple as that sounds, we do things that betray that simple logic every day. Like buying something we can't afford with money we don't have and creating a debt that we will find difficult to repay. Like spending money we do have foolishly when we should be saving it. Saving for retirement as soon as possible has other benefits. Just as a longer gun barrel makes for a more accurate shot, a longer investment horizon makes for higher returns. The decade that began with the year 2000 is sometimes called the "lost decade" for U.S. stocks because of the volatility of the stock market. Once you iron out the peaks and valleys of that 10-year span, you have what is essentially a flat growth line. During the previous decade, however, the American economy recorded the longest uninterrupted period of expansion in its history. What's the point? Given a longer time horizon, the returns of any investment, even one with which risk is associated, is usually better. The lost decade, with its two record-setting market crashes, is a painful reminder of how market performance can deviate from historical averages when there is volatility. But time has a way of smoothing things out – a factor that will work to benefit of those who have time on their side.

If you save early, you will have the freedom to pursue potentially lucrative job opportunities that come your way even if there is a temporary financial hit to your income. If you save early, you won't fight with your family about money decisions. And if you save early, you definitely won't be up late at night worrying where the money will come from to pay for all those upcoming bills. You can choose to improve your lifestyle as you age instead of feeling like you are always making sacrifices by downgrading your lifestyle as your obligations increase. Too many people spend their younger years living large, only to be forced to downgrade as they age and start a family. If you save early, you won't be used to a larger lifestyle in the first place and due to your outsized savings, you can choose to upgrade your lifestyle as you see fit.

Christopher Columbus and the Penny

When Christopher Columbus sweet-talked Queen Isabella into funding his journey to discover the New World in 1492, history was made. You probably read all about it in elementary school. But let's imagine that Columbus found a penny on the sand when he finally made it to the Americas. And let's say that he put that penny in his pocket and as soon as he could get to a bank, he deposited it at 6% interest. And let's also say that ol' Chris forgot all about his little investment and just this year his descendants discovered the account. Take a wild guess at how much would be in the account. Would you believe over $121 billion? That is the power of compound interest.

I discovered this illustration in 2009, which is 517 years from 1492. If you wish to check the math, just get out your calculator and multiply $.01 times 1.06%, and repeat the calculation 517 times. You should come up with $121,096,709,346.21. It's easy to see why Albert Einstein was so impressed, isn't it?

To demonstrate the power of plowing the interest back into the investment and allowing the interest to compound along with the principal, consider that the penny Columbus found on the beach would only be worth around 31 cents. It's the snowball effect that creates the magic. Time and reinvesting the interest.

The Penny Doubling

Since we're discussing the power of a single penny when put to work, there is another hypothetical illustration that is bound to make your jaw drop. A job applicant was asked whether he would rather be compensated with a straight $1,000 per week, or a penny, doubled every day for a month, at which time his wages would stop for the rest of the year. In other words, he would earn a single penny the first day, two pennies on day two, four pennies on day four, and so on. But after he was paid for that month, he would receive no salary for the next 11 months. If you were offered a deal like that, which option would you select? If you took the "penny doubling daily" pay plan you would have earned a little over $5 million by the end of the month. If you want to check it out, draw a square on a piece of copy paper and make a 30-day calendar out of it. Then take your calculator and start doubling your penny. At the end of the 30 days you will end up with 536,870,912 pennies, or $5,368,709.12. Again, the power of time and reinvested interest.

Take Advantage of Savings Plans at Work

When I see young people opt out of participating in their employer-sponsored retirement savings plans at work, it breaks my heart. Why on earth would you not want to take full advantage of something that could make you wealthy by the time you retire? For 2014, the maximum amount you could contribute from your salary to a tax-deferred retirement savings plan, such as a 4-01(k) or 403(b), was $17,500. If you are just getting by on what you make, it's understandable that you might not be able to take **full** advantage of such a program, but at least throw **something** at it. Saving 10% of your earnings toward retirement is recommended as a starting place. What pains me the most is to see young people spend money on luxuries and non-necessities at the expense of saving? As my father used to say, "You can have the things money can buy, or you can have the money...but you can't have both." In other words, once money is spent, it is gone. The message he was trying to get across to me in those younger days was that savings should come first. Once that priority is satisfied, then spending money is an option.

Some young employees pass up generous matching funds offered to them by their employers, not realizing that they are essentially saying no to free **money!** Some employers don't contribute matching funds at all, some match your contributions dollar for dollar up to a percentage, and others match a portion, such as 50 cents for every dollar you put in up to, say 6%, or 3% of your salary. But whatever the amount is it is free money. Why do they do it? It's usually a part of the benefits package offering health insurance and paid vacations. Companies do that sort of thing to attract quality people and keep them happy. It is also a tax benefit for employers. Whatever the motive behind it, employer matching funds speeds up your account growth considerably.

Dollar-Cost Averaging

As we will see in subsequent chapters in this book, the stock market can be a dangerous place for someone approaching retirement. But for a young person willing to invest steadily and consistently over a period of years, the volatility of the stock market can even work to their advantage because of the principles behind "dollar-cost averaging."

Dollar-cost averaging is a simple investing technique that allows you to invest pre-determined amounts of money over time. Let's say you are offered the opportunity by your employer to participate in a 401(k) program, and you contribute $100 per month. That money is used by the custodian of the program to purchase shares of mutual funds. The number of shares purchased will be determined by the price of the shares at the time you make the contribution. What happens if the share price goes up? That's great news! Your investment account just gained more money. What happens if the share price goes down? That's great news too! You just bought more shares. Either way, it's a win/win situation for you. Don't worry, just like grain-fed piglets, those "skinny" shares will eventually "fatten up."

Meanwhile, you are still pumping in the same amount, month after month, and your account does nothing but grow.

Many investors use dollar-cost averaging in conjunction with an automatic investment plan. The key is to put the amount you invest on automatic pilot. Set it and forget it mode works very well for this kind of investment strategy. Over time those consistent, small investments start to add up. Over decades, of course, your investment averages out so you pay an "average" amount for your stocks. Dollar-cost averaging is an attractive way to get started investing with a small amount of money. If you are investing at work, you probably have the help of someone from the Human Resources department. They can guide you through your options. In most cases, you are given a menu of choices that reflect your risk tolerance. Even when young, it is best to balance your investments and spread your risk. Often the third-party custodian who manages the 401(k) program will offer choices in this regard. A financial advisor can usually offer guidance to you in this respect, as well.

If you are investing on your own and aren't able to take advantage of professional investment advice, I recommend that you start with something simple to understand, like an index fund. Keep in mind, that with dollar-cost averaging you are not trying to "time the market" or "pick stocks." You are not trying to get in early on the next Google or Microsoft. You just want to invest in something broad-based that you know will be here for a while. Index funds are representative of an overall slice of the market. The Standard and Poors (S&P) 500 index, for example, has been widely regarded as a reliable gauge of the large cap U.S. equities market ever since it was introduced in 1957. It is called the S&P **500** because it includes 500 companies in leading industries of the U.S. economy, capturing 75% coverage of U.S. equities. Standard and Poor's is a rating agency that does financial research. So, when you invest in the S&P index, you are not picking a company out of the herd and putting all of your "eggs" in that company's "basket." You are investing in the overall performance of a group of companies. Index shares will go up and down, but you will be further insulated from risk of loss by those two principles we discussed earlier – time and reinvestment of the gains.

Live Below Your Means

In America, everyone is entitled to pursue happiness and dream the great American dream of prosperity and financial independence. Sadly, some of us kill that dream by our poor spending habits. Suze Orman is a television personality who is known for her frank talk and flinty approach to finances. She and I don't agree on everything, but I think she nailed it in a 2013 appearance on National Public Television when she said, "You have got to live below your **means** and within your **needs**." She went on to explain: "If you can afford a 2,000-square-foot home, buy a 1,500 square-foot home. If your car is five years old and its running great, but you want a new car, don't buy it. Keep what you have."

She's right about that. If you spend all the money that is within your means, you essentially spend all the money that you have. And if you spend all the money that you have, you don't have any money to save for retirement. There was a time in America when all you had to do was hook a job with a big company, work for them 30 years, and they gave you a gold watch and a nice pension that would take care of you the rest of your life. That just isn't the case today. Pensions are disappearing faster than the polar ice cap. Young people starting their careers today will have to make their own pensions through ardent savings and careful spending.

Avoid Debt Like the Plague

Earlier in this chapter we quoted Albert Einstein's profound remarks about compound interest... "He who understands it earns it, he who doesn't, pays it." Interest, then, is a two-edged sword that slices two ways. You may earn it when you save it, but you certainly do pay it when you borrow. Banks and credit card companies work overtime to entice young couples starting out in life to subscribe to their cards. They offer zero interest for six months as a "teaser" rate and "cash back" or "airline miles." The trap many young people fall into is thinking that they will be able to control their spending, that they will always pay the bill off as soon as they receive it and they will never run up a credit card debt. But it is so easy to just pull out the plastic when you see something you want. And it is so easy to say "put it on the card" after an expensive meal at a fine restaurant. The illusion is that you are not really spending money, when it's worse than that – you are going into debt.

Debt can turn the miracle of compound interest into an ugly curse. If you have a revolving charge account, your debt can approach 25% or more! Banks know what they are doing when they target young people with solid jobs and high credit scores. You are the perfect target. You are starting out in life, so you need things. You are actively involved in discovering all the world has to offer. The free enterprise system loves a buyer. Stores make it easy for you to buy now and pay for it later. If you want to have a retirement harvest, however, you simply must learn to hold up your hand like a traffic cop saying, "Halt!" and learn to say no to credit card debt.

Always Have an Emergency Fund

The last little piece of advice I will give you in this chapter on things to do when you are young to ensure that you enjoy a rich and full retirement harvest, is to have an emergency fund. In fact, an emergency fund is actually the first step to financial success. It starts with a stash of cash equal to at least nine months of your annual income that can be used for, well, emergencies...anything that can come along that you weren't expecting that can cause you sudden expense. You could lose your job. Your car could die. You could get sick. Your house could burn down. You could be hurt in an accident. Insurance for those things is great, but there is usually a deductible. Credit cards are good to have for emergencies, but you don't want to use them for reasons stated in the paragraph above.

An emergency fund must be money that is (a) liquid and (b) readily accessible. The first thought that comes to mind is an interest-bearing checking account or a savings account that earns interest. Most such accounts provide you with automatic teller access.

The psychological importance of having an emergency account lies in the fact that you will not be tempted to interrupt your savings program and dip into your retirement account when something unexpected comes along. Staying on track with your savings is job one if you intend to have a retirement harvest.

Part 2
Summer

Chapter Four

Growing Your Assets for Future Use

> *"He who works his land will have abundant food..."* - Proverbs 28:19

If you have ever grown a vegetable garden, you know the feelings of reward and fulfillment that come from slicing open that first ripe tomato or making a salad out of what you personally produced with your own hands from the earth. Growing a garden is a lot of work. It takes patience, time and sweat to grow your own food. Most people who garden these days don't do so out of necessity; it's more of a back-to-nature hobby indulged in by those with a lot of time on their hands. But in years gone by, especially in rural America, gardening was a necessary activity that put at least half the food on the table.

My mother started our garden on paper first; she made a list of what she would plant. I'm sure she envisioned in her mind's eye how many rows of peas, how many rows of squash and how many rows of "snap beans" (that's green beans to the folks up north) she would have in her spacious garden. For her, the exercise started with a square drawn on a piece of paper.

When the time was right (most experienced gardeners know this instinctively) she, with another family member or two helping her, put the seeds or seedlings into the ground. Then it was simply a matter of protecting it from weeds, pests, drought and predators, and watching it grow. A worry-free retirement starts with similar planning. The earlier we start, the better, of course. But for my friends who have let time pass them by – better late than never. The growing season in North Carolina where I grew up was long and forgiving – more than 200 days. And it was always amazing to me how growth could be accelerated in the rich, sandy soil by the addition of the right kind and amount of fertilizer and proper moisture. So to those who have neglected planning, I say start now. You may not reap as large a harvest, but when it comes to your retirement, some planning is better than no planning at all.

We go through three distinct phases in our financial lives:

- Accumulation (Planting and Growing)
- Preservation & Income (Harvest)
- Distribution / Death (Legacy)

Accumulation – (mid 20s to mid 50s or early 60s) We begin by saving, planting if you will. We contribute to our retirement accounts and begin managing our financial affairs as adults. As the decades roll by during this phase, we crystallize our financial goals. It's during this time in our lives that we usually start families. As we acquire responsibilities along the way, we taste the sense of obligation we knew only vaguely from observing the things with which our parents may have struggled. Our incomes usually increase over these years. Responsible people save and invest for retirement.

When we get into our 50s, things change. Family responsibilities become less pressing for some. The furniture is all paid for and the mortgage is whittled down. The kids are finishing with their education or they are on their own. Time has passed and the money they have set aside for retirement has grown. Consistent saving has paid off and, as the pages of the calendar flutter upward and away, people start thinking more and more about their eventual retirement. Their tolerance for risk is understandably lower than it was in the heady days of earlier decades. Increasingly, they place more emphasis on passive income generation and preservation of capital. It is during this period that prudent investors shy away from risk and volatility. Their life clock tells them it is more important to keep what they have accumulated and allow it to continue growing at a reasonable rate of return, than to risk what they have worked so hard to accumulate in the hopes of accelerated short-term growth. The accumulation phase is a time for trade-offs. The growth/safety trade off. The risk/reward trade off. The spend/save trade off.

Preservation and Income (Harvest) – (mid 50s and beyond) Now comes the final and hopefully the most rewarding and fulfilling phase of your financial life. It is a time for reaping the rewards of all of our hard work and diligent savings. For most folks, this phase of life starts when they retire. The years of the fat paychecks are over, and it's time to circle the wagons and live on what we accumulated and any other sources of income we have in place. For a lucky few, there are pensions. For others there are the 401(k)s, 403(b)s, SEPs or other defined contribution retirement accounts we maintained thorough our working years. We fed those accounts; now it's time for those accounts to feed us. There are dangers in this phase too. We are vulnerable to unexpected health-care costs and premature illness. Unexpected expenses may arise having to do with aging parents and adult children who need our assistance. These things may threaten our financial well-being. This age group is sometimes called the "sandwich generation" because situations arise forcing them to care for family members. This is also the time in their lives when they begin thinking about the legacy they would like to leave behind for children and grandchildren.

This book will focus primarily on the **Harvest** phase of financial life. In my opinion, it is the area where so much can be forfeited by mistakes – errors in handling our accumulated wealth just when we can least afford them. In order to reap a bountiful retirement harvest, we must make good decisions from a wellspring of accurate knowledge. Since this is the area in which I have chosen to specialize with my practice, it is naturally the area with which I am most familiar. But that is not all of it. I am passionate about passing along to you, dear reader, the things I have learned that can ensure you of a worry-free financial harvest.

Retirement means different things to different individuals. The word itself connotes a "withdrawing" from something. But the vision of retirement that modern retirees have is quite different from that of their parents' generation. Instead of a sedentary life spent rocking on the porch and watching the world pass them by, retirees of today seem focused on an active life of travel and personal exploration. This fact adds even more importance to the idea of conserving assets leading up to retirement. If this dream of independent, worry-free retirement is to be fulfilled, the funds must be there to support it.

Summer is Growing Season

Our farm family enjoyed watching Mother Nature work its miracle of growth on the 140 acres we called home. Each year we looked for and witnessed the greening of the fields as the seeds we planted germinated, took root and slowly became big plants. As a kid, it was fun and interesting to observe all of this. It was also the time when Mackey and Ronnie, my two brothers, and I worked the hardest. The plants weren't the only things that were growing. Weeds thrived in the warm sunshine too. Old fashioned mulching and weeding by hand sometimes seemed the most effective. Our hands grew quite well acquainted with the feel of the hoe handle during the growing season. The reward, of course, was that toward the end of the growing season, the growth of the tall, maturing plants overshadowed the weeds and seemed to scare them off. The plants you wanted were now on auto-pilot, so to speak.

During the growing season, a number of things can threaten plants. If the drainage of the field is poor, a hard, prolonged rain can drown your crops or erode the soil. If you don't make provisions for proper irrigation, drought can kill the crop or severely retard its growth. Insects can appear suddenly and render your work useless in a matter of days. Animal pests love gardens and can ruin what you plant if they are not controlled.

Fortunately for farmers, agricultural science has identified most crop threats and university extension services have provided helpful advice on how to contain them. But it is up to farmers to keep up with that science and apply the advice. Those who do so usually reap bountiful harvests. Those who ignore the advice usually pay a price.

Are there threats to your retirement garden? You bet! Plenty of them! And the same kind of diligence is required to keep them at bay. Here are some roadblocks to our financial success that present themselves during the accumulation years and what steps can be taken to prevent them from ruining our retirement harvest.

Taxes – I don't mean the ordinary taxes that we know we owe and don't mind paying. I mean the sudden tax hikes than can strain our finances in retirement. Take a poll and you will find that most people, including experts and analysts, say that tax increases are inevitable in the decades to come. As mentioned earlier, economic changes are like changes in the weather. They are caused by the building up of irrepressible pressures. Statistics indicate a large segment of the population seems to be either unable to, or unwilling to, fund their basic needs. This has resulted in an increase in government subsidies and entitlement programs. In any case, retirees should not assume they will be in a lower tax bracket in retirement. It may not be a bad idea to consider the advantages of Roth IRAs or Roth 401(k)s that provide tax-free income in retirement. A word of caution: See your financial advisor before rushing into a Roth conversion. There are balancing factors that must be considered before determining whether this is in your best financial interests. This is one of the areas that many financial advisors don't seem to understand and fail to put their clients' assets in a position where they enjoy the best tax advantage.

Unexpected travel – Surprise travel can take a chunk out of our retirement savings and put holes in the budget for retirees living on a fixed income. You may allocate a certain amount for pleasure travel but the unexpected trips to attend weddings, funerals and graduations can sneak up on you. It can be caring for an out-of-state family member that causes the wheels of your budget to come off. When you take money from your savings to accommodate such emergency travel, the price paid is dearer since no extra money is coming in. Have an emergency fund for such occurrences. Keep it liquid and dip into it instead of taking the money from an account that earns interest.

Maintenance and repair – Replacing a worn out car or replacing a damaged roof are unavoidable expenses. Life happens, as the old saying goes. Appliances and automobiles don't last forever. When you do your income planning, account for these things and make your investment decisions accordingly. Create a "rainy day" fund for unexpected expenses by opening a separate savings account and contributing to it regularly.

Medical expenses – This is probably the number one threat to a retiree's financial security, and most people don't plan adequately for it. Medicare coverage doesn't include such things as vision, dental or long-term care coverage. You have to make arrangements for these things privately or pay them out-of-pocket. Medicare is great, but it isn't free and there are large gaps between what medical care actually costs and what Medicare parts A and B cover. You should by all means have a private Medicare Supplement policy or, depending on the coverage level where you live, a Medicare Advantage (Part C) plan. Some financial planners suggest that retirees buy traditional long-term care health insurance as a protection, but this can be costly. Traditional LTC insurance used to be the only option available, but times are changing in that regard. A competent financial advisor will be able to point retirees toward newly developed programs the terms of which may be more amenable to retirees who need to make every dollar count. My team likes to look at ways to cover LTC and increase your estate if you ever need LTC.

Longer life spans – Wait a minute! How could living longer be a bad thing? What we mean is that there is a possibility you could outlive your resources. It's just another factor to include in your planning. Like they say...today's 60 is the new 40. Senior adults are living longer and leading more active lives than did their parents. That may require more in the way of income. This blessing of longevity also makes plans that offer a guarantee of lifetime income more appealing than plans that offer mere projections. Most projections I have seen tend to show a retirement of 20 years or so. That may not be long enough. No one I talk to likes the idea of becoming a burden to family members in their old age or losing their independence because they have outlived their savings

Volatility in the stock market – As Bob Dylan sang back in the early 1960s "The times – they are a-changing." It used to be that, given a few see-saws back and forth and a few peaks and valleys in the charts, you could somewhat predict that the stock market would go up and down but always land on its feet. No more. The instability and market volatility has even the consummate optimists concerned. Historians have marked the decade that began in the year 2000 as the "lost decade" because of the two severe stock market crashes. At the time of this writing, the nation is still in the process of recovering from the last one. From 1926 through 2000, the stock market (as represented by the S&P 500) had an annualized return just over 11%. Since then it has had an annualized return below 2%. Most retirees have gotten the message and withdrawn the lion's share of their assets from the risky roulette wheel that the stock market has become. But for those who haven't, market volatility should be a cause for concern.

Changes to Social Security – This one really depends on your age. Those born between the years 1946 and 1955 are probably immune from changes that are bound to happen to the Social Security system. But if you were born after that time, then you may have cause for concern. Changes to Social Security are inevitable. Trustees of the system say it is fiscally sound until the year 2037, but unless changes are made it will be bankrupt after that. What changes? Measures have been proposed to raise the normal retirement age, reduce the benefits and raise taxes. Either all of the above or some combination is expected. Medicare is also facing reform.

Declining home equity – There was a time when seniors who had worked all of their lives to pay down their mortgages could count on the equity in the home always rising. Since the mortgage crisis of 2007 that isn't such a safe assumption anymore. At the end of March 2011, the ratio of homeowners' equity to value was just 38%, the lowest on record thus far. Prior to the bursting of what has been called the "housing bubble," the ratio of equity to value was rarely below 60%. That is just one more adjustment retirees need to make in their outlook. For those who have always expected to be able to deduct mortgage interest from their taxes, that sacred cow may be led away to the slaughter at some point in the future if the rumors coming out of Washington are to be believed. At least it is being talked about as I write this book.

Lack of planning – The worst of all threats to a secure and happy harvest in retirement is simply failing to plan, or planning poorly. I recently saw a survey that said only 42% of American workers have attempted to determine how much money they will need in retirement. Many have a vague idea but haven't nailed it down. The same survey said that 60% of Americans have less than $25,000 saved for retirement. Planning starts when you begin thinking specifically about how much you will need to live on in retirement. Procrastination and do-it-yourself planning are probably the two biggest natural enemies to a bountiful retirement harvest. Do-it-yourself investors usually make decisions emotionally, or are too optimistic. Procrastinators sometimes wait until it is too late.

Chapter Five

Avoiding the Pitfalls that Can Ruin Your Financial Future

"Money is better than poverty, if only for financial reasons." - Woody Allen

When natural disasters wipe out farmers' crops, they can shake their heads and stoically say, "There's always next year." With retirees, however, it's a different story. The harvest they are working for is longer term. It may take all of their working lives to build their retirement nest egg. If an economic disaster occurs, such as a sudden stock market crash wiping out a significant portion of what they have worked so hard and so long to build, there is usually no opportunity to make it back. There is no "next year."

The closer one is to retirement, the less time there is available to make up what was lost. If inordinate risk is what caused the loss to begin with, the worst thing one approaching retirement can do is take on even greater risk hoping to capitalize on a market recovery that may or may not come in time. At the blackjack tables in Las Vegas they call that "doubling down."

It is so much better to avoid the problem to begin with by making sure you are assuming risk in proportion to your age and the years left before retirement.

The Rule of 100

When people sit down with financial advisors, one of the questions that always comes up is, "What is your risk tolerance?" Investors are usually asked to decide whether they are low risk-takers, moderate risk-takers, or high risk-takers. Most people, not knowing what to check, will go for the middle box – moderate. It seems like the most reasonable category. The question sort of reminds me of the one I had to answer at the dentist's office when I went there once for a toothache. I was asked to draw a circle around the number that corresponded to the intensity of my pain – one being the least intense and 10 being the most intense. I circled five. After all, I wasn't crying and I could engage in conversation. But if it had been a one, the pain would not have driven me to the dentist's office (not my favorite place to visit) in the first place.

When it comes to risk tolerance, no one wants to lose money. So before we choose a risk category, what goes through our minds, whether we voice it or not, is, "what are the odds we will lose?" or "is there another category for people who want a good return with no chance of losing?" The question itself suggests that one must take some risk when investing, which is not necessarily the case.

Personally, I prefer to follow a time-honored investing rule known as the "Rule of 100." It is essentially this: Take your age and subtract it from 100. Put a percent sign after that number and that's the percentage of your assets you should have at risk. Conversely, the remainder should be safely invested in such a way that loss of principal is not a possibility.

If you are 75, for example, then you should have no more than 25% of your assets at risk. By the same token, if you are 25, you should have an emergency fund of perhaps 25% completely safe and the rest should be working for you in aggressive investments (at risk with a good possibility of high reward). Young people should take advantage of the fact that time is on their side. Older people should beware of taking too much risk because time is not on their side. The rule of 100 assumes that the market will rise and the market will fall, but it will always rise more than it fell over time. An older investor will not have time to recover from a market ebb when the unpredictable flow sequence starts.

RULE OF 100 EXAMPLE	
Age – 100 = x% This is the percentage of your assets you should have at risk.	100 - 75 = 25% 75% = Safe Investments 25% = At Risk Investments

The rule of 100 is a "rule of thumb." There are other factors to consider, such as one's individual goals and risk tolerance. While not an absolute rule, it should serve to guide our thinking and prevent us from putting too much money at risk in an unpredictable investment environment. Your comfort level is still a factor, but risk tolerance should not be based on sentiment or feeling. It should be based on logic, math and data. What are the statistics? If you examine recent economic history, you will find that since 1952 the American economy has experienced a recession about every 8 to 10 years. In most cases, that is how long it has taken for our economy to become over-leveraged with credit obligations, making it necessary for the Federal Reserve to forcibly remove our hand from the cookie jar by tightening credit. The resulting higher interest rates cause a recession. Recessions last two years or so, followed by a recovery. Then the cycle starts again. Some recessions are more severe and prolonged than others. Some recoveries are longer and slower than others. That seems to have been the case with the recession that followed the 2008 market crash and the recovery that, at the time of this writing, is still underway, albeit painfully slow.

Since time is such a huge factor in all of this, a younger investor should have a much higher tolerance for risk than an older investor.

Natural Disasters – Economic Disasters

Ignoring investing science has led to many becoming victims of economic disasters. By some estimates, the 2008 stock market crash and the ensuing recession cost the U.S. economy $12.8 trillion. While the economic forces that caused that disaster were uncontrollable, the losses experienced by older investors approaching retirement could have been largely avoided had they approached risk with more science and less sentiment.

Most everyone has heard of the great Dust Bowl of the 1930s. One article I read called it the "most extreme natural event in 350 years." When I read that, I wondered what possibly could have occurred in the 1600s that would have been more extreme, but the article didn't elaborate. The fact remains that the1930s Dust Bowl turned more than a million acres of fertile prairie soil in the Midwest into a scoured wasteland. The phenomenon began on November 11, 1933, when a fierce dust storm stripped topsoil from farmland in South Dakota and was followed by a series of similar storms that year. Then beginning on May 9, 1934, a mammoth dust storm lashed the Great Plains for two days, removing massive amounts of soil. Dust clouds blew all the way to Chicago, depositing 12 million pounds of dust. Two days later the same storm reached cities in the east, such as Buffalo, Boston, Cleveland, New York City and Washington, D.C. During the winter of 1934-1935, red snow fell on parts of New England. The calamity wasn't over. On April 14, 1935, known as "Black Sunday," 20 of the worst "black blizzards" occurred across the entire sweep of the Great Plains, from Canada south to Texas. The dust storms caused extensive damage and turned the day to night. Those who lived through the storm reported they couldn't see five feet in front of them. It was after that storm that the press started calling the land ravaged by the phenomenon the Great Dust Bowl of the Midwest, and the name stuck.

It is called a "natural" event, but the cause was not all natural. Much of it was manmade. What provoked those rolling dust clouds was a combination of severe drought, greed and ignorance. Perhaps nothing could have prevented the drought. There were dry-land farming methods but they weren't followed. By the 1930s farm implements had seen a rapid mechanization. Extensive deep plowing of the virgin prairie topsoil in the preceding decade had displaced the natural deep-rooted grasses that normally kept the soil in place and trapped moisture, even during periods of drought and high winds. But without the natural anchors to keep the soil in place, it dried, turned to dust and blew away in the strong windstorms. Hundreds of thousands of people were forced to abandon their farms and move away.

The best account of all of this can be found in the book, *The Worst Hard Time: The Untold Story of Those Who Survived the Great American Dust Bowl,* by Timothy Eagan. Egan collected first-hand accounts from people who lived through it, and his writing puts you in the middle of it so well that you feel a little dusty after reading it.

The Dust Bowl finally ended in 1941 with the arrival of drenching rains on the plains. The rains restored crops and settled the dust. The land there, although sparsely settled, still produces crops. Farmers now use more scientific methods, such as contour plowing, terracing and crop rotation.

The 2008 Stock Market Crash

Just as ignoring the sound science of farming cost those hundreds of thousands who were victims of the great Dust Bowl of the 1930s their livelihoods, millions of Americans saw their savings disappear in the economic windstorm that occurred in 2008. While it is true that the cycles of economic change are bound to happen, we do have control on how much of our money we allow to be affected by them. Just as crop pests or drought doesn't send a press release notifying us of their advent, there was no advance notice of the stock market collapse. No one saw it coming. Not really. But those who followed the science of risk-appropriate-to-age were rewarded. When the markets were soaring, their portfolios enjoyed modest, stable gains. And when the markets tumbled, their retirement was not jeopardized.

The stock market crash of 2008 was the culmination of a number of slow-developing, irrepressible forces. Business was booming on Wall

Street. The economy was chugging along like a steam locomotive whose operators were unaware the bridge was out ahead and they would soon be involved in history's most dramatic train wreck. The DJIA (Dow Jones Industrial Average), simply called "The Dow" by most folks, started 2007 at a healthy 12,459.54. The pulse was strong in January and would inch steadily upward as the months went by. Some warned of something they called a "housing bubble," but they couldn't be heard over the happy music Wall Street was making and waterfall roar of flowing money. Buyers were scrambling to buy up houses and condominiums as fast as the contractors could build them and put them up for sale.

Construction loans flowed like water in a spring thaw and construction companies built on speculation. The free and easy lending atmosphere filtered down to home buyers. Both wholesale and retail lending institutions were in on the party, and the carefree mood spread all the way up the food chain to the mega banks. On the buyer level, all that was required to obtain a home loan was the intention to make the payments. Banks, after all, were in a win/win situation. How could they lose? They had the property as collateral and the value of property would always go up, wouldn't it? Exotic loans were the order of the day. One popular loan was the "No Doc NINA," which stood for no documentation, no income and no assets." Thankfully, it is now extinct. ARMs (Adjustable Rate Mortgages) were popular too. Few gave much thought to the principal of the loan. In fact, "interest-only" loans were created, allowing the home buyer to pay only the interest and none of the principal.

There may have been some in government who were wondering how long the easy-money party could last, but they weren't doing anything about it. By August 2007, however, the "Fed," or the Federal Reserve as it is officially known, began to see a liquidity problem with big banks. The Fed pumped money at the problem by selling Treasury securities. If anyone lacked proof the economy was entering a danger zone, they had it now. The wheels of the economy weren't falling off yet, but they were beginning to wobble. The culprit in all of this was something called "derivatives." Before the banking troubles that began to manifest themselves in the late summer of 2007, few knew what derivatives were. It certainly wasn't a household term. But it would soon become apparent that derivatives were the rust and the termites to the house of cards that Wall Street had been building throughout the housing boom.

A derivative, as the word suggests, is something that is derived, or based on something else. In economic jargon, a derivative is a financial instrument that derives its value from the value of underlying entities, such as an index, an asset or an interest rate. In other words, a derivative has no value in and of itself. Its only value is the value that is *placed* upon it by those who *deem* it to be worth something.

The deeper the auditors probed the big banks, the uglier it got. Guess what underlay the derivatives representing the billions of dollars in loans the mega-banks had made to wholesale banks? You guessed it. The billions of dollars in bad mortgage loans that were made to keep the air in the housing bubble!

Here's what Warren Buffet, who needs no introduction as an investing guru, said about derivatives way back in 2002 in the Berkshire Hathaway annual report for that year:

> *"I view derivatives as time bombs, both for the parties that deal in them and the economic system. Basically these instruments call for money to change hands at some future date, with the amount to be determined by one or more reference items, such as interest rates, stock prices, or currency values. Central banks and governments have so far found no effective way to control, or even monitor, the risks posed by these contracts.... In my view, derivatives are financial weapons of mass destruction, carrying dangers that, while now latent, are potentially lethal."*

Pretty prophetic, wouldn't you say? By bailing out the big banks, the government was forced to accept subprime mortgages, which were the root of the problem, as collateral. What is amazing, looking back, is how reluctant the public was to accept the handwriting on the wall. Even after the August Treasury selloff, the DJIA still rose, ending the year (2007) at 13,264. The cops had raided the party but nobody wanted to go home!

It wasn't until March 2008, after the GDP (Gross Domestic Product) fell to 6% and the jobs report showed that 17,000 more people were out of work that the wheels began to wobble so discernibly that even the most optimistic on Wall Street had to pay attention. It was also in that month (March 2008) that the Federal Reserve stepped in to save the bacon of the venerable old mega-bank, Bear Stearns – the first casualty of the subprime mortgage crisis. Even with the wheels of the economy flying off, the Dow, as if to defy logic, still rose above 13,000 once the Fed's decision to bailout Bear Stearns was announced. It was to be a short-lived reprieve. The thick clouds of economic gloom were gathering thicker and darker.

The next big bank dominos to fall were two government-sponsored entities, Fannie Mae (Federal National Mortgage Association) and Freddie Mac (Federal Home Loan Mortgage Corporation) That happened in July 2008 when the Treasury Department in essence guaranteed $25 billion in their loans and bought shares of Fannie's and Freddie's stock. The Dow dropped to around 11,000. On Monday, September 15, 2008, another mega-bank, Lehman Brothers, went bankrupt. (Ironically, on September 5, 2008 Jim Cramer, the clownish television analyst who likes to use cow bells and zoom whistles to punctuate his stock market advice, told viewers that they should buy Lehman Brothers stock because things couldn't get any worse for the mega bank). Next, the DJIA dropped 508 points. The Fed then bailed another too-big-to-fail conglomerate, American International Group (AIG), which had run out of cash attempting to cover its credit default swaps it issued against mortgage-backed securities. On Wednesday, September 17, 2008, the Dow dropped 449 points, wallowed up and down for a few more days, until September 29, 2008, when it nose-dived 777.68 points – the most in any single day in history. The panic led to a 7,552.29 Dow and the train was careening off the cliff. The Great Recession of 2008 was underway.

Picking up the Pieces

You could say that financial advisors specialize in certain areas of wealth the way doctors specialize in certain areas of health. I specialize in retirement income planning for seniors who are in or approaching that financial phase of their lives. Because of that, I focus on safe-money investing and, because of that, none of my clients lost a nickel in the 2008 Wall Street meltdown – at least not in the portion of their portfolios over which I had oversight. My view is that seniors approaching retirement need to begin turning off all the valves through which their wealth could escape the retirement tank and begin organizing their financial affairs for the distribution phase of their lives. No, the time for accumulation is not over. Their money still needs to be working for them throughout their retirement. But the growth on that money needs to be at a reasonable rate that incurs no risk to principal.

I like to compare your investments to a house. If you lose the roof or the walls you can always rebuild as long as you have a foundation. But if you lose your foundation, you've lost it all.

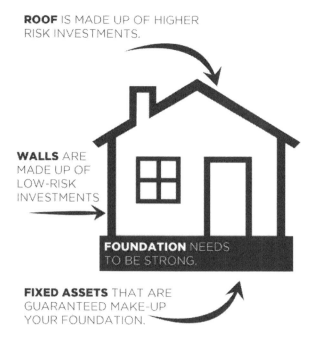

ROOF IS MADE UP OF HIGHER RISK INVESTMENTS.

WALLS ARE MADE UP OF LOW-RISK INVESTMENTS

FOUNDATION NEEDS TO BE STRONG.

FIXED ASSETS THAT ARE GUARANTEED MAKE-UP YOUR FOUNDATION.

There is a Latin phrase: "Primum non nocere," which translates to "First, do no harm." It has long been said to be part of the Hippocratic Oath that doctors take before entering their medical practices. I spoke to a doctor friend of mine and he told me that doctors don't take any such oath – that's just one of those "urban legends" that seem to never die. And besides that, he said the "do no harm" phrase is not even in the Hippocratic Oath. I was a little disappointed. I sort of like the idea of "first, do no harm" when it comes to medical treatment. I think it is a good motto for financial advisors, too...especially those who advise folks on what to do with their money as they approach retirement. I don't think I could roll out of bed in the morning and come into the office if I knew advice I gave to a client resulted in that person losing a substantial portion of his or her savings at a time when they needed it the most. In my opinion, the first order of business in helping a retiree to establish a financial plan is to protect the assets on hand from loss – especially when those assets are non-renewable.

When you read accounts of how the American investing public lost almost $13 trillion in the 2008 market crash and its aftermath, that number is difficult to comprehend. It is so huge, it belies understanding. We sit down to write a check for $100 to pay a bill. We understand that amount. Perhaps you have a goal of reaching a net worth of $1million or more before retiring. We can wrap our minds around that with no difficulty. But unless you are Warren Buffett, Bill Gates or the comptroller of a large corporation, you don't think in terms of billions or trillions of dollars. Just because million rhymes with trillion doesn't mean the value of those two dimensions are anywhere near the same. For example, a billion is a hundred million, but a trillion is a thousand billion! That's quite a leap! To put it in some kind of perspective, a billion seconds is 31 years. A trillion seconds equals 1,688 years! So when you read the national debt is $17 trillion and rising, or the stock market crash of 2008 cost the people of America $13 trillion, you just give a low whistle and shake your head.

As a financial counselor, I was on the front lines during the fall of 2008. While my clients were unscathed, I interviewed several prospective clients during the months that followed the crash and saw the economic disaster in human terms. It was a little like being a first responder at an accident scene. One couple who visited my office in early 2009 lost more than half of their life savings, and they were angry and distrustful.

"Why didn't anyone warn us?" asked the woman. "We would have taken our money out of the stock market."

Both were 62. They had planned to sell the small business they owned and retire at age 64. They had figured the amount of income they needed in retirement down to the penny. Their investments did well during the 1990s, and they felt confident that their portfolio of stocks and mutual funds would fare as well in the decade that followed. Their broker gave them no reason to reposition any of their assets. In all fairness, neither their broker nor any of the analysts to whom their broker had looked to for guidance, had any way of knowing about the coming economic meltdown. In many respects, they were acting with good intentions. They were just like those farmers who kept plowing the same fields over and over just before the Dust Bowl, or the real estate brokers who, before the housing bubble burst, could not imagine property losing value.

There was nothing I could do about the money the couple had already lost in the market. The best thing I could do was to help them stop the bleeding by repositioning what remained in their accounts out of harm's way and develop a plan that would help them recover and would offer some guarantees. Fortunately, the couple was in good health and had no debt. They decided to postpone their retirement, a move they calculated would get them back to the point where they could retire with confidence. Only this time, they wanted their plan to include guarantees and to allow for inflation and long-term health-care coverage.

The Root Cause of Over-Risk

Lack of education is the main cause of investing mistakes such as those made by the couple mentioned above. Wall Street influences Main Street through the media and spends billions of dollars each year to get across its message that, when it comes to investing, risk-taking is the only way to financial success. The bias expressed in the print media and over the television cable channels is quite apparent to those who are knowledgeable in the area of safe-money investing. Some come on the tube and put forth the notion that the stock market is the only place to put your money if you want to grow it, and they have the uncanny ability to pick which stocks will win and which ones will lose. The truth is no one can predict such a thing – not long term, anyway. And if you wonder why magazines articles or television shows cast negative aspersions on investing strategies that don't fit within their no-risk/no-reward mindset, you have no further to look than the advertisements that fuel such articles and TV shows. Brokerage houses make money whether you win or lose in the market. Mutual fund managers charge the same fees regardless of the direction your investment takes. The media seems to love it when people predict the future. It makes for excellent theatre and interesting reading. But no one – repeat, no one – can tell you which way the market is going to turn, no matter how many charts and graphs they produce. Charts and graphs tell the past, not the future, and forecasts of the future are best guesses based on the past. Yes, sometimes their predictions are right, but even a broken clock is right two times a day. That doesn't make it an accurate timepiece.

It would be truly wonderful if we could put all of our money in the stock market and buy all the shares of stock we could just before those shares made their move upward, and then sell those shares just before they head south. That's called "timing the market," and it's impossible. Emotions such as fear and greed are what fuel the market. If anyone tries to convince you they have a magic wand or a crystal ball that counters that truth, run – especially if you are nearing retirement. . Stock picking and market timing are both traps. To reap a bountiful retirement harvest, avoid such traps. Follow the investing rule of 100. Save systematically and steadily throughout your working years, but reduce risk as you go. Those wise choices will ensure a solid financial future and a bountiful retirement harvest.

Chapter Six

Retirees and the
Health Care Dilemma

> *"For wisdom will come into your heart, and
> knowledge will be pleasant to your soul;
> discretion will watch over you, understanding
> will guard you."* Proverbs 2:10, *11* English
> Standard Version

No discussion on retirement would be complete without crossing
the bridge of rising healthcare costs. As a financial planner specializing
in retirement, I find myself having to ask difficult questions sometimes.
By very the nature of my profession, I deal with contingencies – the
"what-ifs" of life. If the ultimate goal is to be able to retire with peace
of mind, knowing your bases are covered and nothing can threaten
your income stream throughout retirement, even if it lasts 30 or more
years, then we must look at potential threats to that income stream and
figure out how to disarm them if we can. Preparing for sudden illness
can be a daunting challenge.

The Long-Term Health-Care Dilemma

I know of one couple (Fred and Norma, we will call them) who
recently faced the challenge of placing Fred's 83-year-old mother, who
suffered from Alzheimer's disease, into an extended care facility. Fred
and Norma were in their early 60s at the time, and it made them think
about their own future. When they began exploring the cost of

purchasing long-term care insurance for themselves, they were shocked to discover how expensive it was. The premiums were between $2,000 and $5,000 per year, depending on the level of coverage they selected. The insurance agent told them that, assuming they were both deemed healthy enough to qualify for the coverage, a policy that would provide a total benefit of $164,000 each, based on a daily benefit of $150 for a three-year benefit period, would cost them $4,824 per year. The coverage value of that policy could increase annually because of a 3% inflation option, but that was extra.

They were again surprised when they learned that traditional long-term health care coverage, aside from the expense factor, is like automobile insurance. If you don't use the coverage, you don't get a refund. That money is gone forever. It is essentially a "use-it-or-lose-it" proposition.

Some individuals who bought long-term care insurance several years ago in an effort to protect themselves against rising costs are surprised to learn the premiums can go up. Let's say you keep the policy for several years and the premium doubles from $200 per month to $400 per month, then you are faced with a dilemma. Drop the policy and all of those premiums go down a black hole. Picking it back up again may not be an option if you have experienced a change in your health status. LTC policies are underwritten.

In the face of rising premiums, some compromise by reducing benefits, increasing the elimination period (increasing the amount of time before the benefits begin) or reducing the time for which the coverage will apply if the care is protracted. All of these are difficult choices to make but millions of Americans are faced with them every day.

Insurance company analysts tell us that providers are feeling the pinch as well. According to an article that appeared in the *Chicago Tribune*'s business section on April 13, 2012, entitled "Long-term Care Dilemma," Reuters correspondent Kathleen Kingsbury reported the two-pronged problem of an aging population and the rising cost of health care is putting insurance companies in a difficult position. She says that 10 out of the top 20 carriers in the country had left the market in the five years previous to the time the article was written. She also reported that more than seven million Americans have long-term care insurance and prices on new long-term care plans are 6% to 17% higher than those of the previous year. Some providers, she said, are seeking approval for premium increases of as high as 90%. Ouch!

With the "use-it-or-lose-it" terms of these policies and their skyrocketing premiums, it is no wonder they are not flying off the shelves. Americans are just saying no to long-term care insurance. Insurance companies say they are not to blame for the rate hikes, since they are merely adjusting to higher provider costs. Their profit picture is bleak, too, when interest rates are low, making it more difficult for them to pay claims and still make a profit.

In one press release, John Hancock Financial, one of the largest providers still selling LTC policies, stated, "The long-term care industry is still young and only now is seeing actual usage data, which indicate the need for rate increases."

According to the U.S. Department of Health and Human Services, some 70% of people over 65 will require long-term care of some kind during their lifetime at a cost ranging from $4,000 to $8,000 per month, and persons with more than $2,000 in assets can't qualify for Medicaid assistance.

Many are under the mistaken impression that Medicare covers long-term care. Medicare will only pay for 100 days in a nursing home, and the rough equivalent of that for home health care. But Medicare rules stipulate the payment is only for the time you are receiving what is called "skilled care," which is defined as around-the-clock care needed for a patient to "continue to improve." The phrase "continue to improve" is the determining factor as to whether you even receive the 100 days of care. For example, if you are receiving rehabilitation therapy after surgery, Medicare will cover the cost as long as the rehab is needed *if* you are still improving. As soon as the doctors deem you to have reached a plateau in your recovery, even if it is merely a pause in the process, then you are technically no longer "continuing to improve" and Medicare stops paying – whether you have been receiving the therapy for 20 or 90 days.

So, no, Medicare doesn't pay for long-term health care. Not really. If you do not have some form of long-term care insurance, and if you can't afford private pay, then that leaves Medicaid.

A Personal Story

Unfortunately, I have a personal long-term care experience that I have learned from and I hope you can too. As this is written, both my parents are in assisted living facilities. Both have already had years of home health care. My father's Alzheimer's requires constant care and my mother cannot live by herself because of multiple ailments.

I can hear it now: "Well, since you are an advisor, there should be no problems for your family!" The truth is we did discuss this risk before the fact and we did do some basic planning. But my parents could not be persuaded on some matters of personal choice, and I felt it would be disrespectful to press the issue too much. You may second-guess that if you wish, but I find it very difficult to push family members to spend money in the interest of planning, even when I know it's in their best interests to do so. My parents elected to go the cheapest route. This was also very early in my career, and if I had it to do over again, I may have been more insistent that they do more long-term care planning, regardless of the cost. Heck, if I had it to do over again, I would have come up with the money and paid for it myself! But, like they say, "Hindsight is 20/20 vision."

It is too late to do anything about it now, but let's just say that long-term care is expensive with a capital "E" and failure to plan for it will cost you dearly.

What Are The Chances You Will Need LTC?

Most people still push back on the idea of long-term care planning because they don't want to think it will happen to them. Christine Benz, writer for the popular business website, Morningstar.com, in an article dated August 9, 2012, listed what she called "40 Must-Know Statistics about Long-Term Care" and urged her readers to "arm yourself with the facts on how frequently people need long-term care, how much it costs, and how long it's needed." Here are a few of the statistics she says we should be aware of.

37 million: Number of Americans age 65 or older in 2005.

81 million: Expected number of Americans age 65 or older in 2050.

9 million: The number of Americans over age 65 who need long-term care in 2012.

12 million: The number of Americans expected to need long-term care in 2020.

40%: The percentage of the older population with long-term care needs who are poor or near-poor (income below 150% of the federal poverty level).

78%: Percentage of the elderly in need of long-term care who receive that care from family members and friends.

34 million: Number of caregivers who provide care to someone age 50 or over.

$113,640: The maximum amount of assets a healthy spouse can retain for the other spouse to be eligible for long-term care benefits provided by Medicaid.

49%: Percentage of nursing home costs covered by Medicaid, 2002.

25%: Percentage of nursing home costs paid out of pocket, 2002.

7.5%: Percentage of nursing home costs covered by private insurance, 2002.

79: Average age upon admittance to a nursing home.

40%: The percentage of individuals who reach age 65 who will enter a nursing home during their lifetimes.

892 days (2.44 years): Average length of stay for current nursing-home residents, 1999.

272 days (8.94 months): Average length of stay for discharged nursing-home residents, 1999.

38%: Percentage of nursing home patients who will eventually be discharged to go home or to another setting.

10%: The percentage of people who enter a nursing home who will stay there five or more years.

65%: The percentage of people who entered a nursing home who died within one year of admission.

Five months: The typical length of nursing-home stay for patients who eventually died in the nursing home.

25%: The percentage of deaths in the U.S. that occurred in nursing homes, 2010.

40%: The expected percentage of deaths in the U.S. occurring in nursing homes by 2020.

68%: The probability that an individual over age 65 will become cognitively impaired or unable to complete at least two "activities of daily living"–including dressing, bathing, or eating–over his or her lifetime.

42%: The percentage of individuals in nursing homes who are experiencing some form of dementia.

33%: The percentage of individuals in nursing homes who are suffering from some form of depression.

71%: Percentage of patients with advanced dementia who died within six months of admission to a nursing home.

$73,000: Median annual rate, nursing-home care in U.S.

3.63%: Increase in median annual nursing-home costs since 2011.

4.5%: Annualized increase in median annual nursing home costs, 2008-2012.

$162,425: Annual cost of nursing home care, Manhattan, N.Y.

$60,773: Annual cost of nursing home care, Des Moines, Iowa.

$86,140: Annual cost of nursing home care, Tampa, Fla.

$41,000: Average annual base rate for residence in assisted living facility, 2012.

$20: Average hourly rate for licensed, non-Medicare-certified home health aide.

7 to 9 million: Estimated number of U.S. residents who had private long-term care insurance, 2010.

59: Age of typical purchaser of long-term care insurance, 2010.

79%: Percentage of long-term care insurance purchasers with more than $100,000 in liquid assets.

44%: Percentage of population age 50 or older with more than $100,000 in liquid assets.

$1,831: Average annual premium for long-term care policy purchased by person age 55 or younger, at coverage start date. (Policy provides a daily benefit of $150, four to five years of coverage in home and institutional settings with a 90-day waiting period, and 5% automatic compound inflation protection.)

$3,421: Average annual premium for same policy purchased by an individual age 70-74.

9%: Percentage of long-term care insurance purchasers who let their policies lapse within the first year of purchase.

Those stats may change a little from year to year and the direction arrow for health-care costs seems to be permanently stuck in the up position, but it gives a pretty good idea of what we all face when it comes to this very real possibility in our own lives. As a retirement income planner, I urge you, dear reader, to take this part of the planning process seriously. You can build up your investments up but an LTC storm can and will wipe it out.

WHY LONG TERM CARE PROTECTION
MAKES SENSE?

THIS BOX REPRESENTS ALL YOUR ASSETS.
LET'S SAY IT'S $1 MILLION

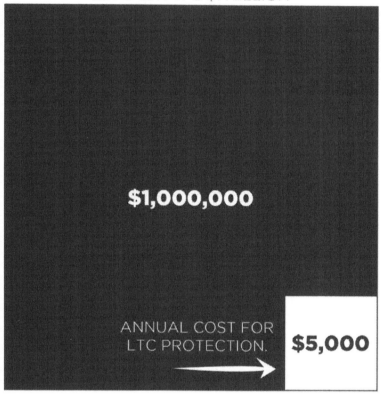

THIS SMALL INVESTMENT OF $5,000
PUTS A PROTECTION FENCE AROUND
YOUR ENTIRE ESTATE.

YOU EITHER PROTECT IT BY TRANSFERRING
THE RISK OR YOU ARE YOUR OWN
INSURANCE COMPANY.

How Medicaid Works

According to some published estimates, seven out of 10 people in nursing homes are on Medicaid. Although Medicaid was created to pay for health care for the poor, many of the recipients of Medicaid benefits are middle-class folks who burned through their savings first, and then, when they qualified for pauper status under the government's guidelines, became dependent on the government for their care. Some of these people were at one time contributing members of society, business owners and entrepreneurs, taxpayers and property owners, but were reduced to indigent status by the high cost of an assisted living facility or nursing home. Some choose to adjust their net worth before they become ill in order to qualify for Medicaid when the time comes. How? By getting rid of their assets, perhaps giving them away to their children, so they can become officially poor and fit the government's Medicaid criteria.

There is nothing illegal about this, but it is not always easy to do. First of all, the government knows this goes on, so they have made it difficult. Any adjustment to your finances with this in mind must follow the strict rules the government has imposed. The "five-year look back" rule is strictly enforced. The objective is to prevent those above the eligibility levels for Medicaid from giving away their resources at the last minute, just so they can qualify for nursing home care under Medicaid. Medicaid is funded on the federal level but administered on the state level. At any time during this look-back period, the state can audit you to determine if any assets, including real property, cash or any other form of assets, have been transferred out of your name. These examiners will be looking for anything of value that you gave away to children or grandchildren, for example, or gifts of money for education or to buy a home or a new car. Unless you were paid full-market value in return for these gifts, the amount transferred will be disallowed and not considered when calculating your Medicaid eligibility.

Some mistakenly think that because the IRS allows you to gift $14,000 per year (as of 2013) to family members without tax consequences, this is outside the scope of the Medicaid audit. Nope. It counts. I have found in dealing with the government on these matters that saying, "I didn't know" or "I forgot" doesn't work very well. It is best to seek the advice of an elder law attorney or a competent planning specialist when you are in this zone.

Many are also not aware of some of the changes that came about as a result of the passage of the Deficit Reduction Act of 2005 (DRA). This dramatically changed the qualifications for Medicaid-funded nursing home care. It is imperative to plan properly with these new rules in mind. Before the DRA became law, the look-back period was three years. Now it is five years. The use of irrevocable trusts can be useful in this regard, but an improperly structured trust is like a boat with a leaky bottom. It will not float for very long when the time comes to use it.

Anyone who has been through this process will understand what the term "spend down" means. An applicant who is close to qualifying for Medicaid, but not there yet, must "spend down" his or her assets according to a list of items allowed. If the money is spent on items **not** on the "spend down" list, then the expenditure will be subject to the five-year look-back. Approved "spend down" categories include such things as pre-paying funeral expenses and replacing an old automobile. But the list is clearly defined and you will need to examine it carefully and hopefully with the help of a professional. It can be tricky.

Possible New Solutions

Insurance companies are in business to make a profit. When long-term care insurance first was developed in the 1970s, it was reasonable and affordable. That was before government regulation forced facilities to improve on the level of their care, which led to increased costs, which led to increased premiums, which led to many declining to buy it, which led to many of the carriers who sold traditional long-term care insurance leaving the market. But since free enterprise abhors a vacuum, the insurance industry began searching for new ways to market policies that would allow them to fill a need for long-term care coverage and still make a profit. Some of these new approaches are quite innovative. Here are a few in brief form:

Combos – This is a hybrid product, hence the word "combo," which is short for "combination." These combine aspects of a traditional fixed annuity with aspects of long-term care coverage. The fixed annuity portion of the contract provides a guaranteed interest rate that is usually more than double, if not triple, what a bank certificate of deposit would earn. The other side of the "combo" is a long-term care coverage that would pay out two to three times the initial policy value over two or three years after the annuity account value is depleted. For example, a purchaser of a $100,000 annuity who selected a benefit limit of 300% and a two-year long-term care benefit factor would have an additional $200,000 available for long-term care expenses, even after the initial $100,000 annuity policy value was depleted. The policy owner would spend down the $100,000 annuity value over a two-year period and then receive the additional $200,000 over a four-year period or longer. In other words, an annuity purchased with $100,000 could potentially payout LTC benefits of $300,000. In that respect, then, it is a fixed annuity and long-term care coverage combined. This product requires a significant, up-front deposit, usually at least $100,000, to make it strong enough to adequately cover health-care costs. Although it has a few more moving parts, it is worth a look. The wording of the Pension Protection Act of 2006 now makes it possible to pay for long-term care benefits from an annuity tax-free. This new approach solves a problem, but it is not for everybody. I recommend that you see a competent retirement planning specialist who is up to date on these contracts so you can examine their suitability for you. Also, while they do not involve the strict underwriting of the traditional long-term care insurance policies, there is usually some underwriting involved. In other words, poor health may disqualify you. But this is a positive trend in the insurance world that has some people saying that it is just what the doctor ordered.

Life Insurance/LTC Combos - To make it simple, the annuity/LTC combo is typically purchased by those who are in good health and who are age 60 and above with some cash to invest. The insurance industry has also designed life insurance policies with long-term care riders. These are becoming popular with those who are under age 80 and are in relatively good health. The reason is because life insurance premiums get higher as you get older. You usually buy these policies with a lump-sum deposit called a "single premium." Like the annuity combo, the premium is usually one-third to one-half of the death benefit. The long-term care benefit is usually around 2% of the death benefit per month.

Here's an example. John buys a life insurance/LTC combination policy and pays a $50,000 premium for a $100,000 death benefit and a long-term care rider. The cash value (not the surrender value) is approximately $50,000. The long-term care benefit would be approximately $2,000 per month if needed. One important caveat: whatever money is paid out in long-term-care benefits reduces the policy's cash value by that same amount. Again, not for everyone, and there is a degree of complexity to these solutions. But from where I observe the ever-changing scene, they are a much better approach to solving the long-term care cost-and-coverage dilemma than that provided by traditional long-term care insurance.

If you have lived any time at all in the adult world, then you know that nothing is perfect and nothing is free. But with these policies the buyer will get some benefit from premiums even if he or she doesn't eventually need long-term care. Either you use some, or all, of the long-term care benefits or **someone** receives a life insurance payment, or you enjoy the proceeds of the annuity growth, or you pass it along to your beneficiaries.

LIFE INSURANCE/COMBO PLAN

- This strategy will cover more than one risk including Long Term Care if needed.
- Let's say we have Mr. and Mrs. Jones with the following Income and assets:

Mr. Jones SS income:	= $1,500 month
Mrs. Jones SS income:	= $1,000 month
Mr. Jones pension income:	= $2,000 month
Investment Income:	= $1,600 month
Total:	= $6,100 month or $73,200 year

$500,000 INVESTMENT ACCOUNT

PROBLEMS:

- Mrs. Jones loses $1,000 month in SS and $1,000 in pension if Mr. Jones dies.
- That's $2,000 month or $240,000 over the next 10 years.
- They also have No Long Term Care.

SOLUTIONS:

- Life Insurance/Combo Plan
- Take $10,000 per year to pay premium from investments.

Benefits are:

- $300,000 Tax-Free Death Benefit to Mrs. Jones.
- $50,000+ in Long Term Care coverage for up to 4 years (Tax Free).
- Death benefit would replace loss of income.
- Possible growth of account value depending on structure.

These types of plans can really make sense and cover many risks.

Not All Policies Are the Same

Are all combination policies the same? No. Not all insurance companies are the same. Check the ratings. Ratings, such as those provided by A.M. Best, Moody's, Standard and Poors or Fitch, for example, are independent evaluations of an insurance company's financial soundness. Remember, too, that that's **all** they are. They do not measure the company's willingness or capability when it comes to handling claims. Nor do ratings measure the level of customer service. They are not the end-all measure by which to assess an insurance company, but they are statistically driven indicators that should be looked at when making a decision.

Next, there are the actual benefits versus premium comparison. Here is a real comparison provided by the American Association for Long-Term Care Insurance of two policies from two leading insurance companies. In each case, analysts compared policies for a 65-year-old married female. The initial policy requires a $100,000 single payment.

Policy A would pay a Death Benefit of **$193,906** and a monthly long-term care benefit of **$8,079.**

Policy B would pay a Death Benefit of **$150,121** and a monthly long-term care benefit of **$6,255.**

Policy C would pay a Death Benefit of **$165,997** and a monthly long-term care benefit of **$5,533.**

Those differences are significant, so it pays to seek the help of a professional who knows how the gears work in these products and can make sure you get the most in the way of benefits for every dollar paid in premium.

With so many new options available, I'm going to go out on a limb here and say there is no longer an excuse for not planning for the very likely possibility of long-term care. Sure, your children will be there to help you, but they can't give you 24-hour care. It would be unfair to expect them to. Kick procrastination to the curb and face this dilemma head on, folks. Just **do it!**

Confusing Medicare Health Options

I was driving home from a meeting a few weeks ago, listening to a call-in talk show on the radio. The subject was Medicare. The caller was a doctor. She was complaining about the complexity of the Medicare program.

"I'm a very educated woman, and I can't make heads or tails of it," she said. "I don't know how the average person can ever hope to understand it." I couldn't help but laugh, not that it's funny, but it's ironic that what was meant to help the elderly and infirm (and don't get me wrong, the program does do that) should be packaged in such confusing language and be so difficult to understand.

Let's face it. Do you know of any program designed by, administered by and explained by Uncle Sam that is simple? I didn't think so. It is a bureaucratic creation. The regulations associated with Medicare come out of Congress too. They are the same people, you know, who brought us (drum roll, please) the IRS code. So much for any hopes of simplicity.

For example, when you are exploring your options, you will come across "Medigap" insurance policies, sometimes called Medicare Supplement policies. These are sold by private companies but under the scrutiny of government regulation. These "Medigap" policies are not to be confused with Part C of Medicare, which came along in 1997 and was first called "Medicare+Choice." It was later renamed Medicare Advantage. These are managed-care versions of Medicare that are offered by private insurance companies. Medicare subsidizes the private carriers. Advantage plans are designed to partially fill in the 20% that original Medicare doesn't cover. Medigap policies have "Plans" and Medicare Coverage comes in "Parts." There is Part A for hospital stays, Part B for doctor visits, Part C to partially fill in the gaps, unless you elect to have private Medigap insurance, and Part D, which came along in 2006, to help seniors pay for prescription drugs.

Here's a bit of trivia for you. Who was the first American citizen to sign up for Medicare? Former president Harry S. Truman at age 81. As soon as President Lyndon B. Johnson signed the Medicare bill into law on July 30, 1965, a ceremony was held during which Mr. Truman was issued the first Medicare card. The card looks pretty much the same as it always did but the program has changed greatly. I doubt LBJ, if he were alive today, would even recognize it.

```
┌──────────────────────────────────────────────┐
│  ████████████████████████████████████████     │
│                                                │
│              Health Insurance                  │
│  ████████████████████████████████████████     │
│           SOCIAL SECURITY ACT                  │
│  NAME OF BENEFICIARY                           │
│  Harry S. Truman                               │
│  CLAIM NUMBER              SEX                  │
│  488-40-6969A              M                   │
│  IS ENTITLED TO            EFFECTIVE DATE       │
│  Hospital Insurance        7-1-66              │
│  Medical Insurance         7-1-66              │
│  SIGN HERE:                                    │
└──────────────────────────────────────────────┘
```

A survey of people born between 1946 and 1964, released by the National Association of Insurance Commissioners (NAIC), found that only 36% knew that 65 was the eligibility age for Medicare. Twenty-one percent thought Medicare coverage began at age 62; 9% percent said they thought it started at age 67; 6 percent said age 59½; and 28 percent said they just didn't know.

One retiree with whom I spoke recently was shocked to learn that her Medicare Part A, which is basic hospital coverage, didn't cover 100% of her medical costs. She was surprised to learn that it came with co-pays, limits and deductibles. This woman had planned to wait until she reached age 70 before taking her Social Security. She was still working at age 65. She enrolled in Medicare Part A, which would serve as secondary insurance to her group insurance at work. A year later, however, she quit her job and left her group coverage behind. She had no idea that something called Medicare Part B even existed and that she needed it to cover a hospital stay. She was surprised to learn that there was a cost involved of around $100 per month. She thought that if she had Medicare Parts A and B, she would be "covered like a glove" as she had been under her old group coverage at work. Such was not the case.

My advice to her and to any who are approaching this time in their lives is to go to the Medicare website, www.Medicare.gov, and read, read, read. The government has done a pretty good job of making the information available, but it's up to you to parse through it and understand it. The website is good, and there is the free booklet *Medicare & You*, which is a comprehensive reference guide (pdf or hard copy) that is published each year by the Centers for Medicare & Medicaid Services. I must say that the editors of this 140-page guide have done reasonably well in their efforts to take a complicated program and make it simple. Assuming you can articulate your Medicare question, the answer is likely there.

While we are on the subject, let me say this about Part D (for prescription drugs). I am glad we have it. Before we had it, many seniors on Medicare had to make a choice between buying medicine or buying groceries. Part D has solved that problem in large measure. But figuring out how it works can try one's patience. In 2011 there are over 1,000 Part D plans offered throughout the country. Uncle Sam sought to save money by privatizing this portion of Medicare, but there are many cooks in the kitchen, each one with a different recipe for baking the same cake. You will encounter terms like "formulary" and "donut hole." If you don't know what they mean now, you will when you begin using Part D.

Part 3

Fall / Harvest Time

Chapter Seven

Finally! The Golden Years!

*"Look, I tell you, lift up your eyes, and see
that the fields are white for harvest." John 4:35*

When you hear the expression "harvest time," it usually conjures
up happy, positive thoughts, especially for a farmer. That's the time
when those who work hard tending to the crops finally get to reap the
rewards for all their labors. Even for non-farmers the sight of the fall
colors and those long, golden sunsets just puts a smile on your face.
When people talk about their "golden years," a similar idea comes to
mind. They have worked hard all their lives and now has come, at last,
the time when they can relax and enjoy the fruits of their labors. "I've
done for others all my life and now it's **my time,**" as one new retiree
put it.

The expression "golden years" puts me in mind of a ripe wheat
field. I don't know if you have ever seen one, but it is a beautiful sight
for a farmer. Wheat, when it is young, is green and looks like ordinary
field grass. But when it ripens, it turns golden-brown and the tightly
packed kernels on the tops of the stalks bend over with the slightest
breeze, causing the entire field to become a golden, rippling ocean.
The head of the wheat plant usually holds between 50 and 60 small
kernels that cling to the top of the stalk as it grows. To any observer,
it's a pretty sight, but to a wheat farmer, it's even prettier because that's
his money out there in that field. He has managed the growth of his
crop with skill and care, and he has defended it from predators and

drought. Now, in a few days, he will be rewarded for all of his hard work.

As a financial planner who specializes in retirement planning, the words "golden years" start me thinking about that phase of life I often refer to as the **preservation** and **income** years.

Preservation – Keep what you've got. This is no time to lose it. Your wealth is now a non-renewable resource. It is no time to play fast and loose with it. You are in conservation mode, not accumulation mode. Sure, you want your money to continue working for you, earning interest, increasing exponentially. But you realize that it would be unwise to take on more risk than necessary.

Sandy's dad, Henry Patrick Vaughan, Jr., standing proudly beside of his tobacco crop.

Income – During your accumulation years, when you were working, you depended on your weekly or monthly paycheck to pay bills and meet expenses. Now that you are retired, that paycheck has to be made up of other sources, such as Social Security, your pension and personal savings. Hopefully you will lead a long and productive life in your "golden years," so your income must have the staying power to last the rest of your life. The alternative is to outlive your resources.

Think of a Tape Measure

Decisions you make at this stage of the game are critical. Some of them, most of them, in fact, cannot be reversed if you choose incorrectly. Financially speaking, you've come this far; you don't want to mess up now. The last two sections of this book will be the "meat and potatoes" so to speak. Our focus will narrow, like a laser beam. We will zoom in on the "what," "where" and "how much" elements of these decisions you now face.

Why is this a critical phase? I saw many people who were badly hurt in the 2008 stock market crash because they invested their assets as if they were in the accumulation phase (spring/summer growing season) of their financial lives, when they were actually in the preservation and income phase (fall/harvest season) phase. The results were devastating.

Whenever I speak at public events, such as seminars and workshops, I like to use a simple illustration that you will easily identify with if you have ever used a tape measure. The kind of tape measure I'm thinking of is the kind with the retractable metal tape that is curved on the underside with inch and foot markings on the top. The inch markings represent the years of your life. Pull the tape out of its holder until the inch mark matches the age when you started working. How old were you? Eighteen? Twenty? Twenty-five? I'm talking about your first official "paycheck" job. Click down the hold button at that age. That was the start of your **accumulation** years.

As you release the hold button and continue extending the measuring tape it's easy to imagine those inch marks as the years of your life sliding by. Sixty...61...62...63. When do you plan on retiring? Sixty-four? Sixty-five? When you pull the tape out to the inch mark that represents the age at which you plan to retire, press the stop and lock button. Now you have entered the **preservation** and **income** phase. During the **accumulation** phase you worked and saved. Now, however, if you are like most Americans, your Social Security will not be nearly enough and you will be depending on your savings and other income sources to generate a paycheck. The financial dynamics of your life have changed in other ways too. Take your risk tolerance, for example. If you still have the tape measure out, extend the metal tape away from the cassette to your life expectancy. We are living longer these days, so give it another 30 inches or so. Is the tape still rigid? Or has it buckled and collapsed? If you are careful, you can extend the measuring tape quite a ways from the cassette and it will remain horizontal. And that's the point. You must be careful. If you want your assets to last you the rest of your life, you must be careful with them. Slow and steady wins here. Extend the tape too far, too fast and gravity takes over. The tape sags, then bends and then buckles under its own weight.

If the pressure of gravity represents market risk, then you get the point of the illustration. The further out you go in retirement, the less market risk you should take on or you may collapse your portfolio. In the preservation and income phase, it's even more critical to manage those assets properly.

One of the tasks of a retirement planner is to help clients determine how much they need to have saved in order to generate the income they will need when they retire. Each case is different, of course. Lifestyles will vary from one couple or individual to another. Therefore, every number will be different. That is why there is no cookie-cutter, one-size-fits-all solution to this as some may have you believe. Every plan must be customized and every strategy or combination of strategies used to accomplish that plan will be "tweaked" to fit the circumstances.

How long will the preservation and income phase last? Until you move into the final phase of your financial life, which is the **distribution phase**. We will go deeper into these weeds further on in the book, but distribution planning can begin before death or it can all happen after death and decisions you make while you are alive can have a dramatic impact on your loved ones for generations to come.

Chapter Eight

Know Where You Are...Financially

"If you don't know where you're going, you might not get there." ~ Yogi Berra

In the autumn of 1849, a wagon train with 200 emigrants from the Midwest were trudging westward through Utah toward the California gold fields where they were sure fortune awaited them. They had all heard of the ill-fated Donner party, most of who had perished after being trapped by the snow of the Sierra Nevada Mountains two years earlier. Seeking to avoid a similar fate, they took a short cut to the south that led them through a barren California salt flat that they had no way of knowing was the lowest, driest and hottest area of North America. Those who survived did so only by first slaughtering their oxen and then staggering westward for days without food or water. Appropriately, they named the place "Death Valley." Does it sound like a bad place to get lost? You bet it is!

Death Valley is a tourist attraction these days, drawing approximately a quarter million visitors each year who brave the sweltering heat to photograph the glittering salt flats. In July 2010, Donna Cooper, 62, her 17-year-old daughter, Gina Cooper, and 19-year-old Jenny Ching Tze Leung, a friend, got lost in Death Valley when their GPS (Global Positioning System), which they had nicknamed "Nell," malfunctioned and sent them down one abandoned dirt road after another until their car ran out of gas. Authorities found them a day later, exhausted, hot and thirsty and with a few choice words for "Nell," their little electronic directions giver.

"You Are Here"

When it comes to investing, it's important to know where you are in the stream of time. If you are young, working hard and saving at least 10% of what you earn, you can do no wrong. You've got the world by the tail and the future looks pretty rosy. If you continue those habits of hard work and arduous saving through your middle years, it gets even better. But once you pass the ol' "double nickel" as they say, things change. The further down the road you get to retirement, you have to be more careful with your assets because once you cut the umbilical paycheck, those assets become non-renewable in a hurry. Forgetting where you are in the stream of that financial timeline and making a wrong decision can have serious negative consequences. In my career of helping people with their finances, I find the one thing that hurts folks the most is that they forget that simple truth.

So, do you know where you are currently? If you go to the shopping mall and you don't know where a store is, you walk up to the directory, you look on the map of the mall and you find a big red X that says, "YOU ARE HERE." Now you can find your destination. Knowing where you are is key.

If you're reading this book, you are probably contemplating retirement. And if that's the case, you are probably about to enter the preservation/income phase. Whether five years away or only one month away, you have a decision to make. Are you going to go it alone or seek the guidance of a professional?

I am reminded of the story about a person going on a trip. They have been offered two choices of air travel. One plane is piloted by a trained aviator with years of experience, fully accredited in the operation of the modern jet aircraft and familiar with each of the knobs, dials and switches in the cockpit. The other plane is equipped the same only without the pilot. This is a do-it-yourself plane. Aboard this plane is a laptop computer and a connection to the internet. All you really need to know about flying the airplane can be found in the instruction manuals and on the internet. You have no lack of information. It's all at your fingertips. Which option would you choose? Obviously the former. It's not the information you need so much as it is the experience and expertise. It's not so much the knowledge you need so much as it is the **applied** knowledge and wisdom that results.

While I am not yet retired, I feel as if I have retired 1,000 times or more through the clients with whom I have worked over the years.

But let's say you are an exception. You really are capable of navigating through retirement by yourself. You still must ask yourself what happens if something were to happen to you? Is whoever you leave behind capable of replicating what you do? More importantly, will they be inclined to do it?

I often encounter husbands who are confident, self-reliant men – traits to be admired. Sometimes they want to do everything pertaining to the family finances on their own. I always ask them if their spouse shares the same enthusiasm for this independent approach. Most of the time, I find the answer is a definite NO. If that's the case, why not at least select an advisor and test them out to see if you want to trust them with your affairs **just in case** something happens to you – someone who is capable of making sure that your plan is carried out if something should happen to you. You could split the money up. You continue managing part of the portfolio the way you choose and allow the retirement specialist manage the rest. You will know very soon if you have found the right person to advise you on your finances. Most experts agree the very worst time for someone to be making major financial decisions is right after the loss of a spouse.

It Gets a Little "Tricky" Here

The other thing about the preservation/income phase of one's financial life is that it is much trickier than the accumulation phase. I didn't make that up. That's what the American College of Financial Services says. Here's an example of what you don't want to happen to you:

84

A couple came to see me in the early part of 2009 and told me their story. In 2007, they had around $500,000. They were told that they could pull 5% out of their account each year and never run out of money. So they started pulling out $25,000 each year in 2007. By the time they came in to visit me, their portfolio was down to almost $250,000. What a nightmare!

I told them that in order to work with me they would have to get the cash outflow down to a manageable figure. If they continued taking $25,000 out per year as their counselors had instructed them, they would be taking out 10% per year. There was another problem. The husband and the wife were only in their mid-sixties. They were on track to run out of money in just a few years.

We put together a plan to lower their risk and lower the amount of their withdrawals. I could not tell them that this plan would stand the test of time. I would love to give you an all hearts-and-flowers ending, but the truth is it is still a sad story. The couple had to lower their standard of living in order to cut back on expenses. They forfeited their plans to travel and had to abandon many of their dreams they had prior to their retirement.

I use this example to underscore the prudence of using guaranteed income as part of the foundation of any sound retirement income plan.

Know Your Options

In summary, you need to know your options and what you can control. The term "financial advisor" is a widely used handle for lots of people in the financial services industry and it is very general in its application. It can mean a lot of things. Find out if the candidate you are considering for your advisor works with every age group or if he or she specializes in the retirement and income phase. That's such an important question that I would like to build it in big block letters 20 feet high, spray paint it with Day-Glo orange and put neon around it. If you are nearing retirement or in retirement and you ask that question and you discover that the advisor candidate does **not** specialize in retirement income planning, you may find out the hard way that you are on a plane with an inexperienced pilot. That may not turn out so well for you.

It's also very important to ask the advisor you are considering trusting with your financial affairs how his or her retirement clients fared and how their accounts performed in 2008. Did they lose a little? Did they lose a lot? Did they gain? The advisor candidate may not be able to answer specifically about an individual client, but he or she will know exactly what you mean and will be able to answer the question in general terms. Don't forget to ask them if they are a fiduciary or are they a registered rep that follows the suitability standard. Are they fee-based? If they are not fee- based, that could be a clue that they are following the suitability standard.

While you are at it, ask them how much each mutual fund cost, both disclosed and undisclosed, amounts to. Ask them if there are 12b-1 fees. Ask them exactly what the trading costs will be within the fund. If they can't forthrightly answer these questions, then walk away.

Ask them if they or their company makes money on a trade. If they do, then walk away. Ask them if they work for only one company, such as a bank or a brokerage firm. If they are independent, ask the name of the custodian they use. Ask if their company has ever been part of a mutual fund lawsuit. According to the book, *Lies About Money* by Ric Edelman, just about every big brokerage firm has been part of a lawsuit.

These questions are not impertinent. They are not intended to be impolite. They are all essential to your ascertaining whether you are dealing with a retirement specialist or a general practitioner. They are necessary to enable you to determine from whom you will take financial advice. They will lead you to the **who** piece of the financial advice puzzle.In the next chapter, we'll explore many of these questions in more detail.

Chapter Nine

The WHO – Finding the Right Advisor

"He that is walking with wise persons will become wise."
Proverbs 13:20 New World Translation

Why can't I just use the same advisor that got me to retirement? What's wrong with using the same people who set up my company's 401(k) retirement plan? They seemed to know what they were talking about. Hey! I've got a toll-free number here for Vanguard!

If you are thinking that way, you are correct in your assumption that those mega-brokerages have advisors standing by, ready to read their script.

Do I really have to explain why not? In the May 2011 issue of *Smart Money* magazine, there was an article featuring this very topic. In summary, it said that it is probably not a good idea to use the same advisor that got you **to** retirement to get you **through** retirement. That would be like continuing to seek medical treatment and advice from your pediatrician once you become an adult.

But how do I find the right advisor?

When I am asked that question by those who attend my educational seminars, I like to explain that the one thing they can control is the **WHO.** The person from whom you take advice is the most crucial element in the decision making process when it comes to selecting a financial advisor. First, find out what **type** of advisor he or she is. Are they accumulation advisors who specialize in investing your money during the time of your life when you are in your working years? Or do they specialize in retirement income? There is a huge difference between the two.

Secondly, find out what are the **standards** to which they are held. For example, are they held to a **fiduciary** standard?

What's that?

In the financial services industry, "fiduciary" is a legal term that has to do with the obligation of a financial professional to ensure that his or her motives for providing counsel and advice to clients are not in the least influenced by personal gain. By legal definition and by ethical and professional standards, a fiduciary works solely for the client. The term "fiduciary" comes from Latin word "fidere," which means "to trust." Keep in mind, this is not a decision that an advisor makes on a case by case basis, nor is it the product of a request that the client makes. A fiduciary advisor is <u>legally bound</u> and <u>contractually obligated</u> to give his or her client advice that is in the client's best interests and not motivated by profit. Fiduciaries are not allowed to be self-serving in their counsel.

Does that mean that they don't receive payment for their services? Not at all. But it is against the law for them to let that remuneration for their expertise and counsel influence or interfere with their advice on a matter pertaining to your financial affairs. In other words, they are not salespersons. They are professional counselors whose obligation is to you and you alone. They have to tell you what is best for you even if they do not benefit one bit. Brokers typically offer investment products not specialty counseling in income planning. You must remember that retirement brings with it unique situations and special challenges. If you are approaching retirement, or if you are already retired, you need a specialist.

In the medical community, I've noticed that doctors quickly refer you to another physician if the need for this is apparent. Go to a general practitioner with a heart problem, and they will without hesitation refer you to a cardiologist. If the problem has to do with cancer, you will be referred to an oncologist. In the financial services community, however, stockbrokers and mutual fund salespeople are known to sit across the table from someone with the special needs of retirement and continue "treating" them as if they were still working, as if their financial station in life had not changed one iota. The discussion will still center on that individual's return on investment, not the preservation of the assets and the income allocations that are needed from it. Why is this? Because brokers are typically not fiduciaries, their natural tendency is to focus on commissionable transactions. Anyone can hang out a shingle that reads "Financial Advisor" but it doesn't make them a fiduciary. True fiduciary-level financial advisors will take a comprehensive approach. They will ask more questions of their clients than non-fiduciaries. They are more likely to discuss strategies and solutions, and they are less likely to talk about products. Most of all, they won't try to sell you anything. You don't get the "wink-wink, nod-nod, have-I-got-a-deal-for-you, get-in-on-the-ground-floor" routine when you discuss your financial affairs with fiduciaries.

When it comes to guiding retirees through this phase of their financial lives, there's a lot more to it than just picking stocks or buying mutual funds. This is a time when you cannot afford a big drawdown on your portfolio. Since you are no longer receiving a paycheck and no longer contributing matched funds into a 401(k), you are no longer the beneficiary of the principles of dollar cost averaging as described in chapter three of this book. Time is no longer on your side when it comes to recovering from a severe market correction. There is absolutely no room for error now. You've got to make sure this money you have worked so hard at saving lasts for another 35 years.

"But I won't live that long"

A centenarian is a person who lives to or beyond the age of 100 years. In 2012, the United Nations Population Division estimated there were 316,600 living centenarians worldwide. According to the U.S. Bureau of the Census, as of 2010, the United States had the greatest number of known centenarians of any nation with 53,364. All of that is interesting, but what is even more fascinating is the **trend.** The 1980

U.S. Census reported only 32,194 people over 100 years of age. The Department for Work and Pensions released a report in 2011 detailing life expectancy in which it compared generations at 20, 50 and 80 years old. The data sees 20-year-olds three times more likely to reach 100 than their grandparents, and twice as likely as their parents.

So how long will you live? That is X the unknown. We are born a book with blank pages and no one knows when our final chapter will appear. Since that is the case, most of the illustrations and projections we run for clients will carry their age out to 100 and beyond. I wish I had a dollar for every time I have heard someone exclaim, "But I won't live to be 100!"

My standard reply is, "Well, at the rate you're going, you will." It may be said tongue in cheek, but more people have those "five generation" pictures on their fireplace mantles and hallway walls than ever before. You just never know.

How many people do you know who are in their eighties and nineties? I am reminded of this phenomenon each time I visit an assisted living facility. Not only is the population of America aging, but the quality of life is improving with it. More and more of the country's senior citizens can and do maintain their independence for longer spans of time than in past decades. If anyone is in doubt of this, talk to an elder care specialist or visit a local assisted living facility or nursing home. It may be a worthwhile field trip for a dose of reality in this area.

Fiduciary Versus Suitability Advisors

Now that we know what a fiduciary is and what a fiduciary does, what is the difference between an advisor who adheres to a fiduciary standard and one who adheres to a suitability standard? And does it matter?

The suitability standard says only that an advisor must do what is *suitable* for an investor. So what's wrong with that? Nothing! It's just not always enough. Think about it this way: When a broker recommends that you buy or sell a particular security, the Securities and Exchange Commission (SEC), which regulates securities dealers, dictates that the broker must have a reasonable basis for believing that the recommendation falls within the bounds of suitability. The broker must consider the client's income and net worth, other security holdings, risk tolerance and investment objectives. But the suitability standard doesn't dictate that the broker necessarily do what is **best** for you. What if you are an older investor seeking income? Your broker isn't required to say, "You know, you have almost all of your money in the stock market. It may be best for you to place at least a portion of your portfolio in a position that is completely risk-free."

Suitability also does not preclude conflicts of interest. Here's an example: There may be two investments that would meet the standards of suitability. One would pay the advisor a 2% commission, and the other would pay him or her a 6% commission. In which direction do you think the advisor would point? The fiduciary standard on the other hand, would require an advisor to eliminate commissions or any other form of remuneration from the process. The Investment Advisers Act of 1940 requires registered investment advisers (RIAs) and their representatives to place the client's best interests above their own. The bottom line: It's important for you to ask your financial advisor which standard they adhere to. No true professional will be insulted if you ask them how they are paid. It's just part of your due diligence in choosing a financial advisor carefully.

Here's another example of how the suitability standard alone may not be enough to protect you. Let's say Joe and Mary bought a bond fund because their advisor told them it was safe. When that bond fund lost 10%, they didn't understand why. The broker, after all, said that the bond fund was "safe." The first lesson here is that it would be a good idea when talking about your money to determine the definition of "safe." If your definition of safe means "no possibility of loss," but to the advisor "safe" simply means "low risk" or "very stable," then, as the crew of Apollo 13 radioed down to their ground crew, "Houston, we have a problem."

But in this case, the product is "suitable" according to the legal definition of the term. You agreed to it and you read the prospectus; that's all the seller of that bond fund has to worry about.

Something else to consider is that a mutual fund is managed to a **prospectus,** not an **objective.** Some folks say they feel they are diversified because they own a mutual fund. Let's think about that. If you own a large-cap mutual fund and large cap stocks get hammered, then you will get hammered. A large-cap mutual fund has to own large-cap stocks because that's what the prospectus says it must own. The fund manager must manage to that prospectus. They can't go to cash when a market correction happens, such as the 2008 meltdown. They must stay the course.

Bottom line: Every advisor is either held to the stricter **fiduciary** standard or the less strict **suitability** standard. The fiduciary standard says that an advisor must always do what's in the client's best interest. The suitability standard means merely that the financial product is suitable, not necessarily the best for the client's objectives. Every advisor falls under one of these two standards. It's up to you to decide which one is for you. I know what you're thinking – "Why, fiduciary, of course!" But would it surprise you to know that a significant portion of the financial advice given and followed these days falls under suitability standards? It's true. There has been a push to make the higher standard uniform among financial professionals. But the big brokerage firms and the mutual fund industry have fought back on this, and as of this writing the uniform standard has not become the law of the land. The argument has been going on for years.

Products versus Professional Planning

When I first began my career in the financial services industry, I worked for one company. I don't wish to throw rocks at anybody, but it didn't take me long to realize that I was nothing more than a product salesman for this one company. I only had access to their product toolbox, which, of course, restricted me. I knew that I could not help my clients holistically working for one company. It was as if I were a mechanic and when people brought their cars in for me to repair, I was restricted to a screwdriver and a pair of pliers to do the job. I had never been so professionally frustrated in all my life. When you work for the big company, you have to answer to them first, not the client.

That, too, didn't sit well with me. After a few years of that, I left Great Big Company and started my own independent advisory firm. I became a totally independent advisor with my own registered investment advisory firm. I partner with a great custodian, Fidelity Institutional. They offer my firm custodial services, but they allow me to be completely independent. In effect, they put a fence around your money and no one can cross that fence except you.

Most of the large brokerage firms and banks push certain mutual fund families because they have revenue sharing agreements (a fancy way of saying "kickbacks") with them. Some of these big brokerages and banks create their own mutual fund. Talk about a "conflict of interest"...Holy Cow! Some even disclose this on their websites and documents. But the consumers don't suspect a thing. These companies fly blimps over the Super Bowl and run television ads non-stop. Many of their corporations are household names. In the mind of Joe Public, they must be the best, right? No, Joe, they're not. They just have a blimp and plenty of money to spend on ads.

Recommendations with Hidden Fees

Big brokerage firms love to sell mutual funds, even to clients who are in the no-risk zone of retirement. They often tout mutual funds as the ultimate in diversification and proclaim them as the means by which to attain to wealth and financial security. Most people who buy mutual funds never read the fine print and fail to ever realize the many hidden fees lurk within. Here's a multiple choice question for you:

A 12b-1 is:
> (a) A long-range strategic bomber
> (b) A vitamin usually administered by injection
> (c) A useless, hidden mutual fund fee that costs
> mutual fund investors billions of dollars each year.

If you answered "C" you may have what is behind door number #1, which is the just the beginning of an education as to how expensive in the way of hidden fees these popular (over $11 trillion owned by more than 90 million individuals in the U.S.) * investment vehicles actually are. If you think 12b-1 is an odd name for a fee charged by a mutual fund, you are not alone. It was named for the 1980 rule of the Securities and Exchange Commission that authorized mutual fund companies to charge companies and individuals when they buy fund shares. Mostly they go to pay agents and those who sell the funds. So call them commissions. Commissions are okay. We don't expect these salesmen to work for nothing, but the problem is that (1) these charges reduce the funds' return and (2) they are not advertised and spelled out to consumers. It is a ridiculous trading cost that even the *Wall Street Journal* has described as unfair. A WSJ article appeared May 1, 2010 entitled, "The Hidden Costs of Mutual Funds." It claimed the average expense ratio is 1.31% of assets each year. More importantly, the article said that the average trading costs are .44% with many that go up to 2.96%!

Some do-it-yourself investors think that because they use discount-brokerage "fund supermarkets" to buy and sell funds there are no fees involved. It may be there are no transaction fees, but that doesn't mean the operators of "mutual fund supermarkets" don't get paid. Karen Damato, in another WSJ article on July 6, 2010, entitled, "What are 12b-1 Fees Anyway," reported the following: "When the investor holds shares of a fund on one of those firms' 'no transaction fee' platforms, the fund and/or its manager typically must pay 0.4% of the value of those shares to the firm each year. Many of the funds, in turn, charge investors a 0.25% 12b-1 fee to partially cover that cost. (Why not the full 0.4%? Because a fund can have a 12b-1 charge of up to 0.25% and still call itself a no-load, or no-commission, fund.)"

Interesting, huh? And I am confident it falls into the category of "I didn't know that" for millions of mutual fund investors out there. And that's not all. According to Damato, when funds are sold through full-service brokerage firms, fund companies often charge investors a 0.25% 12b-1 fee and use the proceeds to make payments to the brokerage firm for its services. The individual advisers at the firm also get a piece of the action "for their continuing assistance to investors." That 12b-1 fee can be **in addition to a front-end load**. Issuers of some fund shares, usually identified as Class C shares, compensate the selling company and broker solely through a high 12b-1 fee, often 1%.

What about 401(k) plans? These 12b-1 fees often show up there as well and are used to make payments that help cover the plans' administrative costs. The point is these **products** are often recommended by "financial advisors" who are not fiduciaries because they are not in a position to offer strategies and counseling. If the only tool you have to work with is a hammer, then every problem becomes a nail. Choose your advisor well. The decision you make in this regard could earn you or cost you thousands.

If you want a thorough understanding of how mutual funds work then ask for my FREE recent white paper pictured here that will explain it all in detail.

Chapter Ten

Salting Away For Future Use

*"Ants are creatures of little strength, yet they
store up their food in the summer." Proverb
30:25 New International Version*

Before the days of refrigeration, farm families canned vegetables in
glass jars with vacuum lids. They preserved meat using various time-
tested methods that included salting, spicing, smoking, pickling and
drying. That way, the family farm was a self-sustaining unit of industry
and consumption. Very few items had to be purchased from the store.
What wasn't consumed during the growing season was "put up" or
preserved for winter. If those foodstuffs were stored and preserved in
the right manner, they could last a farm family through the roughest of
winters.

It is an apt comparison to preparing for retirement. Of course, the
time to "salt away" money for our golden years of retirement is when
we are in our income-producing and accumulation years. But where
we place those assets can make the difference between a comfortable
retirement and one filled with worry. Once you understand that you
have moved from the accumulation to the preservation phase of your
economic life, action is needed to move your assets away from
accumulation strategies to preservation strategies.

Earlier in this book, we talked about what a win/win situation
dollar-cost averaging is for the younger employee who is contributing
regularly to a 401(k) retirement program. Why can't they lose?

Because if the market goes down, shares are cheaper and they are buying more of them with their monthly contribution. If the market goes up they win again because their account just grew in value. But if they leave their money in the same account once they retire, what happens then? They now become victims of the same process that benefitted them so well for so long. Call it **reverse** dollar-cost averaging. What was at one time their regular **contribution** to the account now becomes their regular **withdrawal**. Let's face it, their expenses are the same each month. They need to make withdrawals in the same amount each month to meet those expenses. They must withdraw the funds from their retirement account regardless of the movement of the stock market. When they were in accumulation mode, each contribution to the account translated into share purchases. Now each withdrawal translates into the sale of shares. When they were in accumulation mode, those "skinny" shares they bought when the market was down would later fatten up when the market rebounded. Time was their friend. Now the process is reversed. They are removing shares that no longer have that opportunity to "fatten." Once sold, they are gone forever.

Although that may be as obvious as a full moon on a clear night to some people who retire, believe it or not, millions of others retire and leave their retirement account with their former employer. Why? Probably because it is easier to do nothing than to do something. I call it being the victim of inertia.

The law of inertia is one of Sir Isaac Newton's three basic laws of physics. In essence, it says that an object in motion will continue in motion unless acted upon by an outside force. The same principle applies to an object that is stationary. At some point, the thought may cross the retiring employee's mind that he should move that 401(k) account, but days fade into weeks and weeks into months and months into years and it never gets done.

According to an article by Kevin Cimring that appeared July 26, 2013, in *Fox Business* magazine entitled "Orphaned 401(k)s: Are You Leaving Money on the Table?" the average American holds more than seven jobs in a lifetime. "All too often, workers neglect their 401(k)s as they move from job to job," he says.

Personally, I think failing to monitor such a valuable asset is imprudent. Professionally, I think it is reflective of how little in the way of education corporate fund managers provide to their employees. Why get stuck with high-risk investments that do not meet your current investment needs, risk tolerance and overall circumstances? I recommend rolling over your 401(k) to a self-directed IRA account over which you will have full control. It is unwise to cash out the account unless you absolutely have to have a lump sum. You will have an immediate and possibly severe tax burden if you do, and you will lose the future earning potential of the portfolio, which doesn't make a whole lot of sense if you are trying to fund your retirement.

A word of caution regarding early withdrawals from any 401(k) or other tax-deferred retirement account. This option will prompt a 10% penalty if you're under age 59 ½, not to mention the higher tax bill you will pay on the withdrawal. Think roll-over or transfer, not cash out, if at all possible.

Chapter Eleven

Income – The Key to a Comfortable Retirement

"Wisdom is a shelter as money is a shelter, but the advantage of knowledge is this: Wisdom preserves those who have it." ~ Ecclesiastes 7:12
New International Version

On our family farm, the best part of winter was waking up on a cold, windy day to the smell of fresh-baked biscuits and a jar of sweet peach preserves. My brother and I would slather on the butter, scoop a heaping spoonful of jam and chew slowly as this "winter delight" tickled our taste buds. Sometimes I'd catch our mother smiling at us. I'm sure that part of her joy arose from seeing her boys devour her delicious delicacies. But in retrospect, I also believe that she felt *comfortable*, knowing that she and my father had preserved enough foodstuffs in the cellar, pantry and freezer to care for our needs throughout the winter.

In fact, because winter naturally brought an end to the work in the fields, we had more time to relax and meditate. As a child, I remember being mesmerized by all the jars in the pantry. We had red jars filled with tomatoes, beets or strawberry jam; green jars filled with pickles or green beans; and purple jars filled with grape jam or plums or berries. To a kid, it seemed as if those jars would never run out. But to my parents, this stockpile was finite and, therefore, they carefully monitored and meted out the produce according to a pretty well-defined plan. But even at that, winter time was not worry time. It was a comfortable time to mend the fences, visit with family and pursue personal interests.

Winter on our North Carolina farm wasn't that long. Predictably, we had 200 days in our growing season – the number of days between the last and first frost. That meant winter only lasted about 165 days. Just to give you some perspective, the state of Michigan has an average growing season of only 150 days and a subsequent "winter" of 215 days. Just for the fun of it, I checked out the growing season in Alaska. As you might guess, it's short! Alaskans have only 100 days to grow their crops, and then they have to preserve enough food to last for a whopping 265 days of "winter."

What would our family have done differently had we been notified that our winter would be extended by an extra 30 days? If we got the news early enough, we would have probably planted more crops in the spring. I'm sure our mother would have added to what she preserved. Sure, it would have meant more work all around – planting, cultivating, harvesting and preserving – but I'm confident Charles and Ruth Stephenson would have done whatever it took to make sure we were prepared, whether it was providing more resources or carefully preserving what we had.

Prepare for a Longer Winter

As we documented in chapter nine, Americans are living longer. Unfortunately those extra years are not inserted into our working years; they are tacked on during autumn and winter of our lives. This single fact that Americans are living longer is creating one of the most profound retirement challenges in history.

Forbes magazine staff writer Ashlea Ebeling, in an August 10, 2012, story aptly titled "Americans Clueless about Life Expectancy, Bungling Retirement Planning," quoted consulting retirement expert and actuary Cindy Levering as saying, "Just planning for *a certain period of time* and not having a contingency plan for living longer is a big mistake."

In a press release dated July 30, 2012, the Society of Actuaries released findings from their 2011 Risks and Process of Retirement

Survey Report that shows increasing longevity as a major retirement planning risk. "Four in 10 retirees and pre-retirees underestimate their longevity by five or more years," the report stated.

"Underestimation of life expectancy, combined with having too short of a planning horizon can result in inadequate funds for retirement needs," Levering said. "There is a general misunderstanding of what 'average life expectancy' means, and when people are told they will live to an age such as 80 or 85, they don't realize that this means there is a 50 percent chance that they could live past that age."

If this is true, a lot of people will be headed to the pantry during the winter of their lives only to find empty shelves. According to the 2007 mortality data, if a male has already lived to be 65 and is enjoying "average" health, he has a 40% chance of living to age 85. It's even better (or worse, if you don't plan) for women. Under these same circumstances, a woman has a 53% chance of living to be 85. When the Allianz Life Insurance Company of North America released the results of their "Reclaiming the Future" survey on June 17, 2010, they revealed that 61% of those surveyed (ages 44-75) said they had a greater fear of outliving their assets than they had of dying.

Don't Be Scared—Be Prepared!

Remember the couple mentioned in Chapter Eight who had originally salted away $500,000? Unfortunately, they were told that they could pull 5% out of their account each year and never run out of money. So they started pulling out $25,000 annually. By the time they came in to visit me, their portfolio was down to almost $250,000. They were on track to run out of money in just a few years. My team was able to "stop the bleeding," but they had to forfeit their "dream retirement" and hunker down for the long winter. Sadly, had they come to me sooner, an appropriate amount of their original $500,000 could have been invested in guaranteed income as part of the foundation of a sound retirement income plan. We'll talk more about that in the next chapter. The best way to deal with the retirement fear of running out of money prematurely is to *plan* it to death. So what are some practical things that you can do to insure that you don't outlive your assets?

Reduce Your Standard of Living

Many who have come face to face with this new reality have had to make changes. Accounting Giant Ernst & Young LLP released a report in July 2008 entitled "Retirement vulnerability of new retirees: The likelihood of outliving their assets," which stated: "The analysis finds that almost three out of five middle-class retirees (annual income prior to retirement between $50,000-100,000) can expect to outlive their financial assets *if* they attempt to maintain their current pre-retirement standard of living."

So if you can't maintain your current standard of living – by how much do you need to reduce it so you don't outlive your assets? According to the EY study, on average, you will need to cut your standard of living by 24%. That may be bitter pill to swallow, but for a new retiree it may just bring the peace of mind that the risk of outliving your assets is now reduced to a negligible 5%. In other words, you have a 95% chance of maintaining this new standard of living for your entire lifetime.

For near-retirees, age 58, with plans to retire at age 65, it is recommended that you begin **now** to reduce your standard of living by the same 24%. Simultaneously, you'll want to plow that savings into your retirement account for the next seven years. Like the new retiree, this will reduce your risk of outliving your assets to a mere 5%.

However, both of these examples assume that you have a defined benefit pension plan provided by your employer. As you know, employer provided pension plans are going the way of the dinosaur, which complicates retirement planning. That is why you want to consult a retirement income specialist in the retirement planning profession as early as possible when planning your retirement.

A Rose By Any Other Name...

In the Allianz study mentioned previously in this chapter, when consumers were asked to describe the ideal financial product for their retirement, 69% said they wanted a product that was guaranteed not to lose value. That's not unusual. In an informal poll, I find that most people who have lived through the market volatility of the 2000s list safety of principle as their number one priority in a retirement plan. After that comes an income they cannot outlive, and then better than average returns.

What's interesting is that they are describing the characteristics of an annuity. And yet in the Allianz poll, when they heard the product they preferred mentioned by name, many voiced distaste for annuities. Why? After a little more probing, it was found that the majority of these respondents had not researched annuities for over 10 years. They had no idea how much annuities and annuity-like products have changed in the last decade. I usually ask people, "Do you dislike the name more than you like the benefits?"

Creating Your Own Pension

In the 1950s, large manufacturing companies in the United States, in an effort to meet union demands and compete for quality workers, began making promises they couldn't keep – at least not continue keeping. In those days it was considered good business to keep an employee working for 30 years. Times have definitely changed. Instead of retaining a "family" of workers, corporations try to farm out much of the work to independent contractors. The once paternalistic corporations have been shucking responsibility for their retiring personnel and placing the burden back on the shoulders of the workers. *Kiplinger*'s September 2011 newsletter, under an article entitled, "Pensions: Take a Lump Sum or Not?," quotes a Government Accountability Office report as follows: "More than half of all private pension plans in the U.S. are either frozen (meaning workers retain benefits they have accrued but no longer earn more) or are closed to new employees."

As of this writing, only one-out-of-three near or recent retirees are covered under a defined benefit plan. These fortunate few may not realize the outstanding value of their plan. Taking a second look at the Ernst & Young study cited above, a married man earning pre-retirement income of $50,000 automatically cuts in half his risk of "outliving his assets" if he is covered under a defined benefit pension plan. This model holds true for women as well.

Typically, companies who provide pensions for their employees provide 100% funding for the plan and assume full responsibility for investing the money. The company's obligation to employees is to pay them the defined benefit upon their retirement, usually for life, with options for spouses to continue receiving the income upon the death of the retiree for slightly reduced payments. Most private pension plans do not adjust for inflation. But inflation can add up. It's kind of like a dripping faucet that produces an almost imperceptible flow that adds up over time. According to *Kiplinger*, "Even at a modest 3% rate of annual inflation, your purchasing power could be cut in half after 24 years."

Recent research indicates that when employees are given the choice between guaranteed monthly payments and a lump sum distribution, 70% chose the lump sum. Could this be because they are uncertain about the financial future of the corporation providing their pension? That could be. It could also be that feel they can do better for themselves by investing the lump sum. In some cases, the math supports that idea. Laws have changed that affect the value corporations assign to lump sums, so consult a retirement income specialist in the financial planning profession before making this decision.

401(k)s, 403(b)s, SEPs, Keoghs

In many respects, corporate pension plans and 401(k)-type retirement accounts are polar opposites. With a corporate pension plan, your employer is responsible for making the contributions to the program, investing the funds and providing you with a defined benefit when you retire. But with a 401(k)-type retirement account, the contributions to the plan comes from the employee who is also responsible for investing the funds. There is no guaranteed payout. The value of the account will depend on how well the investments produce. That is why the 401 (k) is called a defined **contribution** plan and the pensions are referred to as defined **benefit** plans. Sometimes with a 401(k)-type retirement plan, the employer will match a portion of your contribution. So a 401(k)-type retirement account shifts all of the responsibility to you. It is your discipline and investment savvy that determines the value of your account when you retire.

Retiring employees usually have three options for their 401(k)s: Take the money in a lump sum, leave the money in the employer's 401(k), roll the money to an IRA. If you are at this junction I strongly encourage you to consult a professional before making a move. Taking a lump sum can result in serious tax obligations, depending, of course, on the value of the account. There can be penalties involved if you are under 59 ½ too. Leaving the money in the employer's 401(k) plan is usually not a wise choice because your old employer can decide to move their 401(k) program to another custodian where fewer options are available to you and you could pay more in fund expenses, which could mean a lower overall return. The old 401(k) could also place limits on future withdrawals or restrict whom you may designate as beneficiary. Perhaps the most significant reason why this would be less than a wise choice is because you, not your employer, needs to maintain control over this asset. Now that you are retiring, you will most likely benefit the most from transforming the 401(k) account to an income stream but allowing the remainder of the account to grow in a tax-deferred qualified account.

Rolling over the 401(k) account into an IRA is recommended for retirees, but which IRA? Where? You have so many options available to you at this juncture in your financial life that it would be downright foolish not to seek professional help.

Just as a farmer knows when it is time to move the crops out of the field and into the barn, there is a time in your financial life when you want to look at your overall retirement strategy and the tax implications for each stream of income, and make a move in the interests of preservation and conservation. You have planted it and watched it grow. You have harvested it. Now is no time to lose it.

If you're a football coach and you are up by four touchdowns going into the fourth quarter, you have the game won. Are you going to throw the ball downfield on every play or are you going to run the ball and make conservative play calls? Of course, you are going to run the ball and play conservatively, ensuring the play clock winds down. Every time you throw the ball, there is a risk of an interception and the clock stops if the pass is incomplete. It's the same with your retirement. If you've already won the game, why take unnecessary risks? Once you have your income guaranteed for life, then it's your choice if you want to take on more risk. The important thing is to make sure your lifetime income plan is in place first.

PYRAMID OF INVESTING

CLIENT AGE 60
RULE OF 100

YOUR AGE

100-60 = 40% RISK

60% HERE

AGGRESSIVE

LEVERAGED HIGH RISK

GROWTH STOCKS AND ETS — **GROWTH**

MODERATELY MANAGED PORTFOLIOS — **BALANCED**

BONDS – STILL AT RISK
CONSERVATIVE MANAGED PORTFOLIOS — **LOW RISK**

40% HERE

MONEY MARKET – CD'S
FIXED ANNUITIES – TREASURY'S

NO RISK

FOUNDATION

- Make sure your foundation is solid.
- Your income plan must be in place.
- Once income plan is in place, you can move up pyramid with other investments if you're comfortable with that.
- Foundation is made up of products that carry NO RISK.
- The rest of the pyramid can be made up of various instruments such as stocks, bonds, ETF's, low cost mutual funds, or REIT's. Still needs to be managed to your risk tolerance.

Social Security

Most people don't look at it this way, but Social Security is nothing more than a defined benefit program that is sponsored by the government. Like a defined benefit plan sponsored by an employer, your guaranteed benefit is calculated by a specific formula based on how long you have worked, how much income you have earned and how old you are when you decide to begin collecting your checks.

When do you turn on the tap and start collecting your Social Security? It's a simple question, but there is no quick and easy answer. What may be the best time for you may not be the best time for millions of other people. To determine the perfect answer requires that we be part financial planner and part fortune teller. But if we do a little research, we can get pretty close once we know how the benefits are calculated. A good place to begin is by going to the Social Security Administration's web site http://www.ssa.gov/myaccount/. "My Account" is a nifty little tool that does all the work for you. When should you apply for Social Security?

Many make the mistake of confusing Social Security with Medicare. They are two very different things. As of this writing, when you turn 65 you may enroll in Medicare. In fact, unless you have other credible coverage, if you don't sign up for Medicare when you turn 65 you face financial penalties in the form of higher premiums later on when you do enroll.

Now that we have that out of the way, you can start collecting Social Security anytime from age 62 to 70 and the later you start, the bigger your benefit. Just how much bigger depends on when you were born. Americans born from 1943 to 1954 have a "normal" or "full" retirement age of 66. They get 25% less than their normal benefit if they cash in at 62 and 32% more than their normal benefit if they wait until 70. (Those born in later years have a slightly higher "normal" retirement age, which means they take a somewhat bigger hit for claiming their benefits early and get somewhat less of a bonus for waiting until 70.)

Let's say you are turning 62 in June 2014 and you earn $50,000 a year. You could collect about $1,027 a month as a single if you retire at age 62. But if you wait until your full retirement age of 66, your check would be $1,442 a month in 2018, or $2,000 a month (again in today's dollars) starting at age 70 in 2022. Let's say you were earning $150,000 per year. Then, the comparable monthly amounts would be $1,888 at 62, $2,568 at 66 and $3,463 at 70. You can go to the website and see your personal earnings history and calculate your own benefit precisely... but that gives you a rough idea. Of course X the unknown is how long you are going to live. If you live to an average age, you'll end up with roughly the same total benefit no matter when you claim. But nearly no one is average. Women live longer than men, but the benefits aren't gender biased. There is a break-even age – that is, the age at which waiting to collect a bigger check pays off. The win-win is to wait as long as possible and live a very long time. But then again, if you need the money in order to live, then obviously you need the money. Since deferring earns you an 8% increase each year you wait, the argument for using your reserves from an account earning less would seem prudent, at least from a mathematical point of view.

In Chapter 13, we'll peel another layer off this onion when we look at the taxation of Social Security benefits. But I think you're beginning to get the idea here. Retirement planning, especially choosing *when* to turn on which taps of income, is something you want to get right. It's like a giant jigsaw puzzle. You can have all the right pieces in the box, but if you don't get to them in the right order you are not going see the "picture" that you're hoping for. Don't guess at this. Consult a retirement income specialist to make sure your retirement comes together to match your vision.

Oh, one final thought about income. Think about working after you retire. I'm not suggesting you work at something that you don't like to do. I mean working – as so many retirees do – because you want to. I've seen it over and over again. People want to stay connected to their communities. I knew an engineer who retired and was glad to be rid of the workplace stress. But just a month into his retirement he began to experience panic attacks. He went to his family doctor and was surprised to hear that this was normal. His doctor explained that for 30 years, this former engineer's body had pretty much kept the same work schedule. Now he disrupted his routine by retiring, and his body responded by "panicking." The doctor gave him three choices. Choice one: Endure the attacks for six months and then likely he would adjust to his new circumstances. Choice two: Take medication for six months to "ease" the anxiety. Choice three: Find an enjoyable part-time job. This man chose option three. He became a part-time security guard at a bank. Almost instantly, he was back in good form. He was meeting people, liked his new routine and had a bit of extra spending money. Just keep in mind that an "unanticipated" job not only affects the flow of money coming in, but also the flow of tax money going out.

Chapter Twelve

Harvest – From Fields to Storehouses

"By your wisdom and deep knowledge you have got power for yourself, and put silver and gold in your storehouses." ~ Ezekiel 28:4 Bible in Basic English

Farming has changed since I was a boy. We planted our fields with one-half bushel of wheat per acre, and we were pretty pleased when we later transported 25-35 bushels of the golden grain per acre to our storehouses. Today, farmers are reaping 50-70 bushels of wheat per acre and, with the new combines, they can harvest enough wheat in one hour to make 70,000 loaves of bread. But one thing hasn't changed. Every farmer knows that when the growing season is done, he must quickly switch gears to get the crops into the storehouses. If the farmer delays, he may lose his entire harvest.

By experience, farmers also know that wheat in the storehouse looks very different in size, shape and location from wheat in the field. For instance, during the wheat harvest on our family farm, golden kernels were separated from the stalk. Both parts of the plant were used, but they were processed and stored separately. This concept – moving from growth to safe storage – is the same for retirees as it is for farmers, but I find that retirees have a harder time making the transition. Maybe it's like the old joke goes, "No one likes change except a baby in a wet diaper!"

Kenneth's friend Nick Dupree, of Dupree Farms, harvests the 2013 wheat crop.

Annuities

Before you turn the page – because you already have an opinion about this – realize that annuities have changed in the same way that combines and storehouses have changed. To begin with, there are several different "types" of annuities, but they all carry the same basic DNA. All annuities share these features:

- Insurance companies issue all annuities
- Annuity benefits avoid probate and pass immediately to heirs at death
- Earnings grow tax-deferred and are taxed when withdrawn as ordinary income
- All FIXED annuities offer guarantees of principal by the issuer

Your grandfather's – and even your father's – annuity was about as basic as reaping wheat by hand. He deposited a lump sum with an issuer and while it grew tax-deferred, he received a guaranteed return of principal and a fixed rate of return. When it came time for retirement, he was given two choices; paychecks for life or paychecks for a certain number of years. If he chose lifetime paychecks and lived a long time, he won. If he died early, he lost. Or rather, you – as his heir – lost, because the issuer kept the unspent balance.

As you might guess, baby boomers weren't about to settle for this kind of an investment. They, of course, liked the lifetime payouts and tax-deferred growth, but felt cheated by the low fixed rates and forfeiture of funds upon an early death. So the insurance companies went back to the drawing board.

Fixed Index Annuity

First, issuers addressed the problem of "low fixed rates." In a fixed index annuity, your returns are tied to the performance of index funds – such as the S&P 500 – and will grow to a predetermined capped limit of, for instance, 6-10%. On the flip side, when the market falls, you retain your gains and never lose principal due to market volatility. Of course, your money still grows tax-deferred until you withdraw funds and then they are taxed as ordinary income. Oh, and boomers demanded no fees and got it! There are no investment fees, no maintenance fees, no hidden fees – no fees. The only fees you would pay would be tied to any bells and whistles you opted for, such as an optional income rider, but we will go into that in a few minutes. And finally, any balance you didn't spend prior to your death is transferred to your heirs and avoids probate. It is taxable as ordinary income, but if you can provide the inheritance, they can spring for the taxes.

More and more, fixed index annuities are being embraced by investment think tanks. *Investment News*, in its February 2014 newsletter, said indexed annuities are gaining in popularity in the low-interest environment of bank CDs and bonds.

Why All the Flak?

If the new annuities are so appealing, why do Wall Streeters historically speak against them? In a nutshell, if I'm only selling oxen, I'm going to tell you all the reasons why they are better for plowing than mules. Wall Streeters don't have annuities in their "tool bag," so they tend to promote what they do have. There is the tendency to under-represent or misrepresent the products they don't offer.

Apparently, a substantial number of near and new retirees are opting for FIAs. According to a 2013 report by LIMRA, a worldwide financial research institute, last year Americans invested a record $33.9 billion in fixed-index-annuities. Now am I suggesting you do this just because "everyone else is doing it"? No. In fact, annuities are not a suitable investment for everyone, and you should always consult your retirement income specialist before you make this decision. But what I am saying is that things have changed and if you haven't looked at the new annuities, you could be cheating yourself.

The Income Rider

When you tack on an income rider to a Fixed Index Annuity, you create an "income annuity" or "hybrid annuity." It's one more example of boomers having annuities **their way.** This little provision gives you access to your account balance while maintaining your lifetime income.

Right off the bat, many of these hybrid annuities come with a bonus feature. Demand is up and companies want your business. So, depending on the issuer, a company may add an 8% cash bonus to the amount that you deposit. So, for instance, if you deposit $250,000, your account value is immediately $270,000.

In the hybrid account, for accounting purposes, you will have an **actual account** and an **income account.** Each account begins with $270,000. The **actual account** growth corresponds to the stock market index. Remember, the growth is capped, usually somewhere around the 6% mark, and the downside is "capped" at zero. In other words, you always retain your gains, even in a bear (falling) market. Many carriers even add on a guaranteed floor – so that in a flat or falling market you are guaranteed up to 1.25%. Projecting this out, if the market was flat or falling for 10 years, your **actual account** would still grow from $270,000 to $305,713.

Now, let's add on the income rider and look at the **income account.** The **income account** began at $270,000 (just like the actual account), but its growth is tied to a stated rate that varies from carrier to carrier, but typically the annual "roll up" rate is about 7% or 8%. Projecting this out, your **income account** would grow from $270,000 to $531,131. Now you can activate your income rider.

Every insurance company has its own formula based on your age, but here is a typical example. Let's say you decide to turn on the income at age 75. Your payout rate will be 6.5% or $34,523 per year for the rest of your life. If you live for another 20 years, you will collect $690,460. That's two and a half times more than you put in!

What happens if you die? Your heirs inherit the balance in your **actual account.** Using the same figures as above, if you and your spouse die after receiving three years of income, you would have received $103,570. But the value of your **actual account** would be $317,321 if it grew at the rock-bottom 1.25% guaranteed rate. That means that your heirs will inherit $213,751 ($317,321 actual value – $103,570 already received). The income rider gives you a win-win retirement. You get a lifetime guaranteed income and your heirs get the difference between what you actually received and the unspent balance in your **actual account.** Of course the income rider is not free, but its cost will likely amaze you. Income riders can be added to an existing Fixed Index Annuity for only a few basis points, typically less than 1%. Some hybrid annuities also offer a Long-Term Care Benefit and other options. I won't address all of these options in this book because ultimately, annuities are not a "one-size fits all" retirement investment. I believe that today, people have very individual needs and they deserve to work with a retirement income specialist who can come to know and honor those needs before recommending a suitable strategy.

Life Insurance as a Retirement Strategy

Today's life insurance policies can do more than simply provide death benefits for our loved ones. Some polices let you accumulate funds for retirement, while allowing cash withdrawals from the cash value without triggering a taxable event or incurring an early withdrawal penalty customary in IRA and 401(k) plans. In fact, these policies became so popular in the early 1980s that three new laws were passed – TEFRA, DEFRA, and TAMRA – to prevent the tax benefits of life insurance from being abused. In other words, investors were now limited in how much they could invest in these policies.

Life Insurance 101

Term insurance provides coverage for a specified "term" (number of years) such as 10 or 20 years. Because it has no cash value and it covers you for a limited period of time, it is the least expensive life insurance. **Permanent** insurance, also known as whole life, is just as the name implies. It is designed to protect you for your whole life...permanently! Both **term** and **permanent** life insurance require premium payments in exchange for a death benefit payable to the beneficiaries named in the policy. But **permanent** insurance accumulates a cash value that can be used for retirement.

In the late 1970s and early 1980s, United States Treasury Bill rates rocketed up to the double digits. Insurance companies slugged along paying only 1% or 2% on the cash values of **permanent** policies. It didn't take boomers long to do the math and devise their own solution. In record number, boomers began to cash in their **permanent** policies. They purchased cheaper **term** insurance, and took the cash value to the bank. Determined to win the boomers' business back, insurance companies created a new **permanent** policy that paid interest – based on US Treasury Bills – while disclosing to the policyholders all fees, mortality costs and charges.

Named **Universal Life (UL)**, this policy allowed **flexible premium payments** so baby boomers could invest more in UL in prosperous years in order to take advantage of tax-deferred growth. At the same time, UL policies allowed policy owners to take low-interest loans at any time without incurring a penalty. Lastly, life insurance benefits would be paid to named beneficiaries **tax-free**.

Boomers were content with this until the late 1980s, when interest rates "normalized" and the stock market began to soar. Preempting another mass exodus, the insurance company quickly created the **Index Universal Life (IUL)**. IUL policy was designed to work like a ratchet. Cash value increased based on the stock market index, but when the market plummeted, their cash value locked and gains were retained.

IUL's merit a serious look as part of your retirement strategy for the following reasons:

- **Opportunity for higher than average returns**
- **Guaranteed not to lose your principle or gains**
- **Contract loans create tax-free cash flow in retirement**
- **Tax-free death benefit for your heirs**

IUL's are not for everyone. Beyond considering your age, health and financial goals, an astute retirement income specialist will also walk you through the following precautions:

- IUL's are long-term investments, designed to be held at least 10-15 years. Cancellation or early surrender fees can be costly.
- The actual insurance or mortality cost of the IUL is deducted from the contract value, reducing the net return.
- Policy rates and fees can change from year to year as deemed necessary by the carrier.
- A contract lapse can trigger a taxable event.

A word about safety: Insurance and annuities are the only investments that guarantee investment principal and offer growth guarantees for the life of the policy. However, it surprises some that no insurance products are FDIC-insured. The FDIC insures **deposits** at banks. It is important to know that even if you purchase insurance or investment products at a bank, these investments are not insured by FDIC. Instead, the law requires insurance companies to cover a minimum of 100% of their liabilities with reserves. Often, when insurance companies list their credentials they will state "**100% legal reserve life insurance company.**" The government also regulates the percentage of assets an insurance company allocates to various investments. As an industry, insurance companies have an outstanding record of safety and liquidity.

Chapter Thirteen

Weatherproofing — Keeping Out the Elements

"Sensible people will see trouble coming and avoid it, but an unthinking person will walk right into it and regret it later." ~ Proverbs 22:3
Good News Translation

Nothing interfered more with my father's good mood than preventable losses on the farm. In his active years, he took pride in doing it right the first time. After we had worked hard and done "everything" right – plowed, planted, cultivated and harvested – if water or critters sneaked in and ruined our stockpile, it could cause consternation. To his way of thinking, losses that occurred after the goods were in the barn could be prevented by anticipating, inspecting and addressing the problem. So I became really good at double-checking to make sure the doors were latched, there were no leaks in the roof and no sign of varmints.

The same is true for retirement income. There are predictable and preventable leaks and predators that can quietly eat away at your net worth, unless you use some "weatherproofing" techniques to keep these elements out.

"Senior Only Tax"

By now, most of you know that your Social Security benefits can be subject to income taxes. Take a peek at the table below. In 1983 during the presidency of Ronald Reagan, Social Security benefits became taxable for the first time. Basically, it was a pretty simple formula. Up to 50% of your Social Security income would be taxed as ordinary income if your annual base income was $25,000 as a single filer or $32,000 as a couple filing jointly.

YEAR	SINGLE	MARRIED
1983	$25,000	$32,000
1993	$34,000	$44,000

Ten years later under the administration of President William Jefferson Clinton, lawmakers raised the ceiling on this tax to 85% for single filers reporting $34,000 and $44,000 for married couples filing jointly. What many don't know is that there is often a simple solution for this.

Reportable income for the purpose of calculating taxes on Social Security benefits includes such things as:

- Income from bank CDs
- Income from tax-free municipal bonds
- Income from pension
- Income from stocks, mutual funds, and other investments
- Income from wages

Formula: Add your modified annual income + ½ **your combined Social Security benefits** + your combined tax-exempt interest. If the sum is higher than the limit in the box, then your Social Security benefits will be taxed accordingly.

You would be amazed, but over the years I've talked with people with as little as $200 "excess" annual income from one of those sources listed above and that was all it took to trigger this tax. Others face a much larger challenge. But here is the good news. And I'm going to tell you up front that the Internal Revenue Service (IRS) is not shouting this from the roof tops, but it is a bona fide legal provision. IF you simply switch buckets – the vehicles holding your investments – you can **avoid** paying unnecessary taxes.

Here is one way to do that. Move a chunk of your assets from taxable to tax-deferred investments. Because you are not yet receiving the income, the IRS does not count this as "reportable income." One of the most popular "buckets" for this purpose is annuities, which we already talked about in the last chapter. Now it is not that you never pay taxes on your annuity gains, but you defer the tax for years into the future when you start taking distributions.

Why isn't everyone "switching buckets?" According to the Federal Reserve *Survey of Consumer Services*, only 25% of Americans have a financial advisor. It is the job of financial advisors to know what IRS Tax Code contains that can help you maximize your income and avoid paying more than your fair share of taxes.

Individual Retirement Account (IRA)

How can you position your IRA in such a way that your heirs get money that might otherwise go to Uncle Sam in taxes? About 40% of Americans own an IRA but in my experience, most of them don't have a clue about how to "stretch" their IRA. Although the information is contained in the IRS Tax Code, the IRS doesn't pay for public service advertisements to educate the public on how to do it.

Note this comparison of a traditional IRA distribution with that of a Stretch IRA:

Traditional IRA Distribution – A man dies and leaves $75,000 in his IRA to his wife. Being prudent, she enacts a spousal rollover to combine this inheritance with her own IRA, further deferring taxes. Over time, her IRA grows to a value of $200,000. Then she dies, leaving the money to the couple's only son, 50-year-old Bob.

Bob does not have the option to roll this into his IRA. Bob is issued a check for $200,000. That money is taxed as ordinary income in the year it was received, pushing Bob into the highest tax bracket. Sadly, the federal government receives $66,000, making Uncle Sam an equal partner with Bob's two children in the inheritance. In other words, had Bob immediately divided the inheritance between his children, **after tax**, they would have each received $67,000.

Stretch IRA Distribution - Let's rewind. Let's say this couple made arrangements to visit a competent financial advisor who was aware of Publication 7004, Section 401 (a) (9) under the heading of Required Minimum Distributions. The financial advisor helped the couple to fill out the beneficiary forms on each of their IRAs so that their heirs would pay the least amount of tax, while experiencing the highest opportunity for tax-deferred growth.

Years pass and then the husband dies. Per the plan, his wife rolled his IRA into her IRA and kept the inheritance growing tax-deferred. More years pass and then the wife dies. She leaves the IRA to their only son. This time, however, the beneficiary form is filled out exactly as the IRS requires for the "stretch" option to be honored. Incidentally, this couple included their son, Bob, in some of the visits with the advisor so Bob could maximize the investments for his own children.

This time around, Bob was not required to receive a check for $200,000, which would have bumped him into a category where he would have been forced to pay $66,000 in taxes. Bob instead received an inherited IRA and directly transferred the $200,000 into this account. When his parents and the advisor met together with him years before he was informed that, instead of accepting the check and moving the money into his cash flow, he should do a trustee-to-trustee transfer to avoid all taxes. Had he accidentally accepted a check, with the full intention of depositing it in the "inherited IRA," the whole plan would have fallen apart and he would owe taxes on the full amount. Whew! As the proverb says, "Knowledge is a protection."

In Bob's case, he was required to take a $5,000 **required minimum distribution (RMD)**, which did give Uncle Sam a little bit of taxes. However, Bob's kids had more growth in their inheritance than the cost of the taxes or dad's bit of spending money. In fact, because Bob's two children were also properly listed as beneficiaries according to the exact wording of the IRS rules (again, it is worth it to get professional help with this), the tax-deferred status of the original IRA "stretched" to include the original couple's grandchildren.

By the way, what exactly does that mean in dollars and cents? By modest projections, that $200,000 IRA that 50-year-old Bob inherited could grow to over $1,000,000 over the lifetimes of Bob and his children. Implementing a "stretch" IRA prevents a mighty big hole from being punched into your "inheritance bucket."

Important Tips for Stretch IRAs:

- Make sure the money is transferred from "trustee-to-trustee." You do not have the typical 60-day window to redeposit the funds from one IRA to another. If you take a check, it will trigger a taxable event and nullify the stretch option.
- If you have multiple beneficiaries, split the heirs into separate inherited IRA accounts so each beneficiary can enjoy maximum tax advantages.
- Pay special attention to the IRA beneficiary form and seek the guidance of a retirement income specialist. This form alone determines who inherits an IRA and whether or not the IRA can be stretched.
- A "stretch" or inherited IRA has to be properly renamed.

Legally reducing and avoiding unnecessary taxes can be about as complicated as tearing apart an automobile engine and then putting it back together. A few people actually *enjoy* it and do it well. We call them professionals! When it comes to planning your retirement strategy and avoiding taxes, it's time to call in a professional.

How to Choose Retirement Income Specialist

How do you find a reputable financial advisor? Virtually anyone can hang out a shingle and claim to be a financial advisor, but not many of them are specialists when it comes to retirement income planning. I suggest that you interview several retirement income specialists and ask each potential advisor these questions:

- Are you held to a fiduciary standard or a suitability standard? (Remember, fiduciary demands that the advisor puts the client's interest first no matter what. The suitability standard says that an advisor must do what is suitable for an investor, based on that investor's circumstances. Notice that the "suitability standard" does not demand that the broker do what is best for you, only that it is "suitable." It also does not preclude conflicts of interest.)

- Are you an independent advisor or are you captive with only one company? An independent advisor will usually have the entire menu of products to choose from. A captive would only have the products that his or her "captive company" offers, which are not necessarily the best.
- As an advisor, how are you compensated? Advisors are usually compensated by fees or commissions. There is a difference. Some products pay higher commissions and can cause a conflict of interest even though they may be deemed "suitable."
- As an advisor, what are your specialties? Does the advisor mainly work in the accumulation phase of life when more risk is the norm, or does the advisor specialize in the preservation and distribution phase that normally begins after age 50 headed to and through retirement?
- How much experience do you have in the industry? What licenses and training do you have?
- Ask for 3-5 references of current clients
- What happened to the investment options that you offered in 2002 and 2008?

By simply asking these questions, you will put the advisor on notice that you are an active partner in the process. Some advisors like that and others don't. But by asking each advisor the exact same questions, it will give you a good indication of how each advisor thinks and communicates. Once you've narrowed your search down to three, go in and meet each one in person.

Sandy and Ken at Boston's Fenway Park.

Colt with a 10-pound bass he caught at the family pond with lil' sis, Ashlee.

Ashlee and my son-in-law, Corey.

Charles Stephenson and grandson, Colt.

Sandy's parents: Henry Patrick Vaughan, Jr. (Jr.) and Dorothylene Welch Vaughan (Dot)

Kenneth's father, Charles Stephenson, first tractor a Farmall Cub.

About 20 years later, Kenneth is driving a Farmall 100 at the age of 4.

An old-stick tobacco barn.

Harvesting tobacco with present-day harvester.

Kenneth's dad, Charles, getting ready to take tobacco to the market. Payday is finally here.

Ken and Sandy out on the farm. My dad proved that hard work pays off. He started farming this farm as a share-cropper and worked hard enough to buy it 25 years later.

Kenneth maps a plan for clients.

Kenneth and staff at Complete Financial Solutions, Inc., office.

Ken and Sandy still love being around the farm. "I've always loved tractors and farm equipment," Ken said.

Kenneth, 19, and Sandy, 18.

Ken and Sandy's children, Ashlee and Colt.

Colt and Ashlee with family dog Rusty. We lost Rusty October 13, 2010, at the age of 13.

Colt and Ashlee at a family favorite spot, Smith Mountain Lake, Virginia, in October 2013.

Chapter Fourteen

Legacy – Planning for Our Heirs

This chapter was written by my friend and team member, James Adcock, a native of Fuquay-Varina, North Carolina, who practices with the law firm of Cumalander, Adcock & McCraw, LLP, and focuses his practice on the areas of estate planning and administration, residential and commercial real property transactions and civil litigation.

ESTATE PLANNING

Typically, death and dying are not favored dinner table topics. But, as the old saying goes, there are two things you can't escape in life: Death and taxes. Instead of avoiding the subject, let's confront it head on. When confronted with the term "estate planning," some respond with thoughts of "that's for rich folks" or "I'll let my children deal with all that when the time comes" or "I'll worry about that when I'm old." In fact, it is important for each and every person, young and old, and in any financial condition to have a plan in place. The planning process does not have to be cold and detached; after all, it should be viewed as a celebration of life and accomplishments and ensuring that future generations will benefit from your life's work.

The following information is for general informational purposes only and is not a substitute for consultation with a competent attorney and no attorney client relationship has been established between the reader and the author.

FAILURE TO PLAN

In the event that you die without a valid will or alternative method of distribution, a plan is in place by default just for you – courtesy of the state legislature. In North Carolina, a person who dies without a will (referred to as "Intestate" or "Intestacy") has certain property distributed pursuant to the terms of the North Carolina Intestate Succession Act. The Act assigns ownership of certain real and personal property to "heirs" that may consist of parents, surviving spouses, children or a combination of the foregoing, depending on which and how many heirs are then living.

Property that is held jointly with right of survivorship, held subject to Transfer on Death (TOD) or Pay on Death (POD) provisions, retirement plans with named designated beneficiaries and life insurance policies payable to named beneficiaries are not included in the "probate estate."

The intestate statutory scheme controls the distribution of items of personal property that comprise the probate estate including, but not limited to: bank accounts, stock, brokerage accounts, cars, collections, boats and household items that are held in the individual name of the decedent.

In addition to personal property, the statutory scheme also governs the distribution of real property held by the decedent, unless the property was held as "tenants by the entireties" (which passes to the surviving spouse at death,) or as "joint tenants with right of survivorship" (which passes to the surviving co-owner at death).

In an intestate estate, the statute contains a list of those who qualify, in order of preference, to administer the estate. This person is referred to as the "Administrator." This Administrator is akin to the "Executor" who is nominated under a person's will.

If a person dies with minor children, the statute further complicates the distribution of the probate estate. In some situations certain property being passed to the minor children will be held by the court until the child is of the age of majority, which is currently 18 years of age.

132

Additionally, bond is required for intestate estates where an heir is a minor. Bond is an insurance policy that protects the heirs of the estate from the misappropriation or mismanagement of the administrator. Bond is an additional expense and the extent of the expense depends on the value of the probate estate. In an intestate estate where all heirs are of the age of majority, bond may be waived with the consent of all the heirs.

Another problem can arise when dealing with minor children – who has custody in the event there are no parents or relatives? This may result in court intervention to make that determination.

THE WILL

A will is the most basic and recognized estate planning document that is part of all good estate plans. It controls the disposition of probate property (as defined in the intestate distribution section of this chapter) at a person's death. The will also nominates an executor of an individual's choosing to administer the estate. Wills may be revoked or amended at any time prior to death.

The most common type of will leaves all property to the surviving spouse and, in the event there is no surviving spouse, to the surviving children. This works in many situations where clients are in their first marriage, and all children are a product of that marriage. This type of will is often called a sweetheart or mirror image will, because the will of the husband and wife have identical dispositive provisions for each other.

Wills may contain alternate provisions in cases where there are children of a prior marriage or no children at all. These provisions must be carefully crafted for the individual situation and goals of the client.

A will often contains a trust provision for beneficiaries, known as a "Testamentary Trust," where a person of your choice will be appointed as "Trustee" to hold and use the property for the benefit of minor children, young adults, persons with special needs, and persons who lack financial discipline. These trust provisions help accomplish goals of preserving property and preventing beneficiaries from squandering their inheritance.

Common trust provisions include giving the trustee discretion over distributions to beneficiaries while staggering mandatory distributions of certain percentages of trust property upon the beneficiary attaining certain milestones, such as reaching a certain age.

The executor is an individual or institution nominated under the will and appointed by the court to administer the estate upon a person's death. Often, the surviving spouse or a child is named as executor, and the common practice is to name a primary and successor executor. It is important to consider a person's abilities, responsibility, willingness to serve and many other personal and practical factors when choosing your executor. The same consideration must go into the nomination of a trustee under the will, if applicable to your particular situation.

Another important will provision is the nomination of guardians for any minor child, in the event both parents die in a common accident, or if the sole parent dies. The court will typically honor the nomination of guardian under a person's will, and this prevents protracted proceedings, especially in those cases where there is no surviving family or where there are family issues that would lead you to desire a particular person be the guardian. It is common for the guardian to also be nominated as trustee over testamentary trusts for the benefit of the children.

It is imperative to note that property held jointly with right of survivorship, held subject to Transfer on Death (TOD) or Pay on Death (POD) provisions, retirement plans with named designated beneficiaries, life insurance policies payable to named beneficiaries, real estate held as tenants by the entireties (husband and wife), and real estate held as joint tenants with right of survivorship ARE NOT CONTROLLED BY THE WILL AND ARE NOT GENERALLY PART OF THE PROBATE ESTATE.

HEALTH CARE POWERS OF ATTORNEY AND LIVING WILLS

In recent years much publicity has been given to end-of-life planning, with headline cases of individuals over whom the decision to discontinue life sustaining measures has been in dispute. State legislatures have subsequently passed statutes that enable a procedure to name a health-care agent and to make decisions in regards to certain medical situations that may occur at the end of life.

The first element is the naming of the health-care agent. This individual is generally a spouse or family member who you appoint to make health-care decisions on your behalf in the event you are incapacitated and cannot make health-care decisions for yourself. Most folks will name two or three, and they will serve as health-care agent in the order named in the document. The health-care agent will have broad authority including the authority to request, review and receive health-care information, employ or discharge providers, consent to admission and discharge from medical facilities, and to consent to medical procedures and treatment. The authority of the health care agent may be limited by the terms of the document, if you have objections to certain treatments or want to include special provisions or limitations.

The second element is the living will or "advanced directive" provision. This provision allows a person the ability to direct that life-prolonging measures be discontinued in certain situations or give the health-care agent the authority to make the decision to discontinue life prolonging measures. Certain scenarios where the decision will be made under the North Carolina statutory language as follows:

1.   I have an incurable or irreversible condition that will result in my death within a relatively short period of time.

2.   I become unconscious and to a high degree of medical certainty, will never again regain my consciousness.

3.   I suffer from advanced dementia or other condition resulting in a substantial loss of cognitive ability and that loss, to a high degree of medical certainty, is not reversible.

Under each scenario, an individual can decide to authorize one of the following.

1. Grant authority to the health-care agent to make the decision to continue or discontinue life-prolonging measures after weighing the benefits and burdens and considering the relief of suffering and quality of life.

2. Direct that life-prolonging measures be withheld in these scenarios. This will remove the authority of the health-care agent to make the decision.

3. Do not authorize health-care agent to make any decision as to the withholding of life prolonging measures and direct maximum treatment to prolong life to the greatest extent medically possible.

Health-care powers of attorney and living wills are sometimes consolidated into one document or are separate documents, depending on the practitioner's preference. These documents can be amended or revoked at any time, as long as the person is competent to do so.

DURABLE POWERS OF ATTORNEY

A durable power of attorney appoints an agent or "attorney-in-fact" to act and perform any act that is outlined under the document. These are generally financial type activities and may include, but are not limited to: collection of property, sale of property, acquiring or retaining investments, managing property, dealing with business interests, borrowing money, lending money, dealing with tax matters, banking transactions and employment of advisors.

The term "durable" means that the authority granted by the power of attorney will continue and not be affected by the subsequent incapacity of the person who executed the power of attorney. This is the primary consideration for powers of attorneys – that your agent can deal with your property and finances when you can no longer do so, due to incapacity.

136

The power of attorney can be made effective immediately or be drafted as a "springing" power, which is effective only upon the incapacity of the person who executes the power of attorney. Additional provisions can limit the agent's power, such as a provision that the agent cannot cause assets to pass to the agent by transfer of property or by changing beneficiary designations.

In the event a person becomes incapacitated and does not have a durable power of attorney, a guardianship proceeding may have to be brought in court to appoint a guardian to manage the property and affairs of the incapacitated individual during the period of incapacity. This may require further court supervision, additional expenses and the possibility that the guardian may be someone the individual would not approve of.

TRUSTS

In recent years there has been an increase in attorneys, financial planners and other industry types who promote a "one size fits all" approach to estate planning, selling you on a handsome notebook full of impressive documents and an even more impressive price. Typically this involves a revocable trust that is proudly marketed with claims of tax savings, avoiding probate and asset protection. Many of these advertised claims can be accomplished by other simpler strategies as well.

The law school definition of a trust is "a fiduciary relationship with respect to property subjecting one who holds legal title with certain equitable duties to deal with the property for the benefit of another" and that, at first glance, is clear as mud. A trust, however, is a simple concept. Cutting through the lawyer speak, property is passed by the creator of the trust (called the Creator, Settlor, Grantor, or Trustor) to the Trustee to be held under the terms of the trust agreement, a written document directing how the property is to be managed and disposed of. The Trustee is an individual or institution who will hold the property and has many duties, called fiduciary duties, among them being the most important duty of loyalty. Because the trustee is holding property of another, he must not use it for his benefit or gain, hence the duty of loyalty.

There are two main types of trusts, revocable and irrevocable. Revocable trusts, as the name implies, may be revoked or amended at any time by the creator of the trust, whereas irrevocable may not be revoked in that manner. This is an oversimplification because North Carolina law allows modifications to irrevocable trusts due to a number of factors and has certain specific requirements to do so, which are outside of the scope of this chapter.

The most common trust for estate planning purposes is the revocable trust. The settlor of the trust is typically the initial trustee as well. The trust agreement typically allows the settlors to take and use trust property during their life and for their benefit and upon the death of the settlor, a provision in the trust is drafted very similar to the will, which outlines the disposition of property, acting as a will substitute. The trust will name successor trustees that will serve in the event of the death or incapacity of the settlor.

Property may be transferred during the settlor's life to the trust, to be managed and distributed under the terms of the trust agreement. It is important that property be transferred into the trust, for the trust and trustee will only control what is held in trust. This means titling real property, stock certificates, bank accounts, brokerage accounts, etc., in the name of the trust. In practice, a will is always drafted and executed to pass any property not held in trust at the death of the settlor to the trust and is commonly known as a pour-over will.

The primary reason cited for the use of the revocable trust as the primary estate planning tool is to avoid probate. So what is probate and what all does it involve?

Probate, loosely defined, is the process of filing the will, being appointed executor, filing inventories of property showing date of death values along with proofs of value, and paying the probate tax and filing fees. Its hardships and costs are often exaggerated by proponents of the revocable trust. Remember a few sentences back we discussed the pour-over will? This will have to be probated if assets exist that are not already held in trust, so now you haven't really avoided anything.

138

In North Carolina, as of the time of the printing of this chapter, the probate tax is roughly .004 times the value of the assets comprising the probate estate. Real estate, whether jointly or individually held, is not included, any joint accounts with right of survivorship are not included, retirement accounts and life insurance policies with named beneficiaries are not included, nor are accounts with pay on death provisions. These assets comprise the bulk of most estates and are not even subject to probate tax. The reality of probate, at least in North Carolina, is not as catastrophic as it is made to seem.

Trusts are also marketed as giving the client immense tax savings. As of printing, the Federal estate tax applicable exclusion amount is $5.25 million per individual, with the ability of a surviving spouse to claim the exclusion amount of the deceased spouse, known as portability, effectively allowing a married couple to pass up to $10.5 million at death with no federal estate tax being due. This amount is set to be adjusted for inflation over time. North Carolina recently repealed its estate tax in 2013. Trust or no trust, the estate tax savings are the same under the current tax, if under the applicable exclusion amount, no estate tax will be due. This is an area that must be constantly reviewed due to the regular changes coming out of Washington and the possibility that the applicable exclusion amount could be lowered.

The other major selling point on trusts is that they provide asset protection. This is a dangerous presupposition that is outright false. Generally, revocable trusts do not provide protection from past, present or future creditors and may result in unnecessary exposure of certain assets to potential creditors.

The classic example of this is the transfer of the personal residence to a revocable trust by a married couple. The husband is involved in an accident and has a judgment rendered against him. His interest in the residence held in trust is fair game to the judgment holder. If the couple held the residence as tenants by the entireties ("John Doe and wife, Jane Doe") outside of trust, the judgment holder could not touch the property.

The purpose of this section is not to bash the revocable trust – it is to temper the claims and exaggerations of certain salesmen. The revocable trust is a useful planning tool, but for reasons other than the common selling points discussed above. Revocable trusts, for example, are useful for individuals with property in multiple states to avoid having to probate in multiple states. Revocable trusts provide a way for assets to be professionally managed during a person's life by institutional or professional trustees. Revocable trusts may also be advantageous for other purposes and should be discussed with competent legal counsel in forming a comprehensive estate plan. There is no one size fits all approach to estate planning.

COMMON MISTAKES

The most common mistakes:
1. Procrastination.
2. Failure to plan.
3. Failure to periodically review and update estate plan.
4. Failure to name beneficiaries on retirement accounts.
5. Do-it-yourself estate planning documents.
6. Failure to update beneficiary designations.
7. Failure to make considerations for minor beneficiaries.
8. Naming a standard revocable or testamentary trust as a beneficiary of a retirement account.
9. Leaving property outright to an individual on governmental assistance.
10. Failure to update plan after divorces.

James S. Adcock III

James Adcock, a native of Fuquay-Varina, North Carolina, practices with the law firm of Cumalander, Adcock & McCraw, LLP, and focuses his practice on the areas of estate planning and administration, residential and commercial real property transactions, and civil litigation. James is also a licensed North Carolina General Contractor and FAA certified private pilot. James is a graduate of Campbell University with a BBA in Trust and Wealth Management. He then went on to attend law school at The University of North

Carolina School of Law. He is a member of the North Carolina State Bar, the North Carolina Bar Association and the Estate Planning and Fiduciary Law Section of the North Carolina Bar Association. James is an active member of Pleasant Grove Baptist Church where he serves as Deacon, and is also active in the Wake County Wildlife Club, Kennebec Flying Club and Military Missions in Action. He and his wife Jennifer reside in Fuquay-Varina.

He may be reached at (919) 552-2929 and jsa@camlawfirm.com.

About the Author

Kenneth Darrell Stephenson grew up in Willow Spring, North Carolina, a small town whose residents will probably always have to explain to folks who aren't from there that there is no "s" at the end of its name. The town's big city neighbor, Raleigh, just 20 miles to the north, has no such problem.

Kenneth grew up on a farm and learned to work hard at a very young age. In fact, he was driving a tractor by the age of six. In those days, if you lived on a family farm, you were just expected to work after school and all summer long. The cash crop in those years was tobacco. In the summer, it was all about placing the harvested leaves into the tobacco barns, an activity which went on from sunup to sundown. Even during the winter months, Kenneth and his brothers cut,

Ken and Sandy in Spain, August 2013. split and hauled wood to customers in Raleigh. The wood was a renewable resource that grew on the 50 acres owned by the family and had to be cleared anyway to make the land suitable for growing crops. Kenneth's father did not want to waste the oak trees, so he started a firewood business that Kenneth and his brothers would run. They ran a small ad in the *Raleigh News and Observer* newspaper that read, "$35 for a truckload of split oak wood" and soon had all the business they could take care of.

Kenneth loved the farm and the life that went with it. "You may leave the farm, but the farm never leaves you," he says.

Of all the milestones that he points to in his life, he says that the "luckiest day" of his life was a Sunday afternoon in July of 1983 when he first laid eyes on Sandy Vaughan.

"The funny thing is that she had dated one of my friends first, so I was reluctant to call her," says Kenneth. But when he realized the relationship with his friend wasn't really a serious one, he worked up the nerve to make what he calls "one of the most important phone calls (or sales calls) of his life." She said, "Yes, I would like to go out with you." Their first date was in the summer of 1983 and they have been together ever since.

Sandy was about to enter her senior year at Harnett Central High School. They were married within 14 months. Sandy was just entering her freshman year of college at nearby Campbell University and many of her friends chided her that now that she was married, she would never finish. But she did. In fact, she graduated magna cum laude with high honors in 1989. She also gave birth to the couple's two children, Colt and Ashlee, while she was a student at the university.

In the meantime, Kenneth had to eventually leave the farm and find his way in the workaday business world. After a few years he settled into the financial services profession. He started out working for one company. The way Kenneth tells it, the first few years were a struggle, but he kept improving.

"The main thing that kept me going was my work ethic, which I had learned while growing up on the farm. I developed the attitude that in order to serve the needs of a client, I would do whatever it took, no matter how long it took to solve a problem and find a solution for someone whose financial wellbeing depended on me."

Kenneth remembers that during his and Sandy's early years raising two small children and working hard to make a start in life, he traveled a lot. He recounts having had an old Jeep Cherokee with at least 350,000 miles on it. It was not unusual for him to drive from one end of the state to the other for a meeting. One particular day he had five meetings scheduled in one day and was just too much for the old Jeep. The vehicle overheated and he was stuck on the side of the road with no money and practically in the middle of nowhere. "I saw a puddle of water and dipped enough water from that puddle to cool the engine down and make it to my meetings and conduct the business I had scheduled there," Kenneth said. "Since I had meetings all the next day as well, I had to stop by an auto parts store, buy a water pump just before they closed, and install it in my yard, in the dark, while my brother held the flashlight."

Kenneth believes that success in anything is an attitude more than it is anything else. "I knew that night, after midnight, after having put that water pump on the motor of that old Jeep, that I was going to make it," Kenneth said. Kenneth became very good at solving people's money problems. He achieved national recognition for his work three years in a row while working for his first firm, all the while attending North Carolina State University and The American College, where he earned his ChFC®, one of the most advanced designations awarded to financial professionals.

Even with the success he was enjoying, Kenneth was also discerning that working for one company offers a problem-solver a limited tool box. He didn't like that. In 2004, he made the tough decision to leave the company with which he had forged so much success and form his own independent financial services firm so that he could work as a true fiduciary for his clients. Now, not beholden to any certain company or dedicated to any one particular strategy or concept, he was free to offer the very best in the way of financial strategies and investments based on the specific and unique needs of his clients. He sought out the best institutional money managers – the ones who would not lose his client's money just when they needed it most. He searched for and established the best partnerships and back office support for his clients.

Speaking of his firm's progress and success, Kenneth said: "It's been amazing so far and we are growing quickly with a definite focus.

144

People are sick and tired of the big brokerages, big banks and big businesses that are too big to fail. People are, at the same time, fed up with Washington and the inability of the congress to get things done. For the first time, many retirees are worried that their children's generation will be worse off upon reaching retirement than was their parents' generation. I believe they want an advisory team that can offer solutions and I think we are doing that. I thank God daily for my best friend and partner, Sandy; my beautiful children, Colt and Ashlee; my background and my upbringing, and the opportunity I have to impact people's lives in such a positive way."

Made in the USA
Charleston, SC
25 July 2014